This book is dedicated to
the loving memory of my mother,
Barbara Corinne Sickles
(1931-1998).
She was taken from us
suddenly and far too soon.
She gave me life
and then enriched it
beyond measure.
Thanks Mom.
I love you.

There are so many people I want to thank that I hardly know where to start. And since it's not the Oscars I can't be hooked off the stage, so don't bother starting the music!

To David Muir, my excellent friend for the last 25 years and my partner in this endeavour. You started the ball rolling and then gave it a kick once in a while to keep it going. Thanks for your great ideas, cool photos and hard work. I look forward to doing this again… soon. Thanks buddy.

Thanks to the gang at The Boomerang Group and Fredrik Carlberg for his funky graphics and the vision to breathe life into this book.

Thanks to Mike Spearman, Francis Ross and Elizabeth Munro for the use of all their really cool kitchen stuff. Did we get everything back to you? Call us and let us know!

To Mike Ingram, my cooking mentor and guru. You've forgotten more about cooking than I'll ever know. Thanks for your inspiration and support.
To Rob Swick and Paul Hernandez, for their constant support and undying friendship. Thanks guys.

To Jill Lambert, Anna Stancer and all the people at Macmillan Canada and CDG Books for believing in this project and for helping this rookie along the way.

And lastly, to Mary Angela Munro and Rachael Munro Sickles for putting up with me and being there for me whenever I needed you. Thanks. I love you both.

Macmillan Canada
Toronto

Canadian Cataloguing in Publication Data

Sickles, Peter
    Pete's Guide to Good Cooking

Includes Index.
ISBN 0-7715-7684-6

1. Cookery. I. Title. II. Title: Guide to good cooking.

TX652.S52 2000   641.5'12   C99-933004-7

This book is available at special discounts for bulk purchases by your group or organization for sales promotions, premiums, fundraising and seminars. For details, contact CDG Books Canada, Special Sales Department, 99 Yorkville Avenue, Suite 400, Toronto, ON M5R 3K5. Tel: 416-963-8830.

1 2 3 4 5 FP 04 03 02 01 00

Macmillan Canada
An imprint of CDG Books Canada
Toronto

Printed in Canada

the basics

TABLE OF CONTENTS

Introduction 4

Part two

a collection of recipes that are pretty darned tasty

it's not rocket science

PETE'S
INTRODUCTION
GUIDE TO GOOD COOKING

This cookbook is more than just a collection of recipes. It's a philosophy. It grew out of my love of good food and my hatred of things that are needlessly complicated.

My name's Pete, and I love to cook. In case you think I'm just a marketing tool, I want you to know otherwise. I'm a 29-year-old (ha ha ha) cook and bartender who lives in the small eastern city of Halifax. I have a bachelor's degree, but have yet to justify the student loan I'm currently paying off. I learned cooking the hard way. My teachers were cookbooks, a couple of friends who are professional cooks and my wonderful mom. Oh yeah, and much trial and error.

There are a couple of reasons that I'm writing this book. First of all, a two of my friends urged me to do it. Marie and Rob kept saying, "This is delicious, you should write a cookbook." Then one day, over a couple of beers, they convinced me to get off my butt and do it. I thought, "Hey, maybe this'll put my writing education to good use. I might even make a little money in the process." Glorious beginnings. Please allow me to ramble for a few moments.

The world is divided into two kinds of people: those who eat to live and those who live to eat. I'm definitely in the latter category. Furthermore, I think that those who eat to live really haven't given eating the attention it deserves.

Eating should be an event. It's delicious aromas and warmth coming from the kitchen. It's sitting down with family and friends. It's conversation and music, good wine and cold beer. It's suddenly realizing that it's 11p.m. and everyone's still at the table.

Sounds pretty good, eh? And you know what? Creating meals that are delicious and that people will rave about isn't difficult at all. You don't need to be a master chef or have a $20,000 kitchen or use all kinds of impossible-to-find exotic ingredients.

When I first started cooking I did so more as a necessity than anything else. Eating out was getting expensive and a little tiresome. I soon found that cooking for myself or someone else could be fun and very rewarding. There's no better way to impress a date than to cook a good meal! I actually got so good at it that I decided to try making a living at it. I've even been moderately successful. I know it sounds cliché, but if I can learn to cook well, anybody can.

My number one kitchen skill used to be licking the spoon when my mom came to visit. After a while I actually found myself giving her cooking tips. Now I regularly cook meals for family and friends. Cooking has become a source of relaxation and a creative outlet. Cooking is not rocket science. I hope this book will help you find enjoyment and satisfaction in the art of cooking. Above all, remember: cooking shouldn't be a chore. Relax. Have fun. Put some tunes on the stereo and crack open a beer or a bottle of wine. Okay? Let's get into it.

chapter 1

CHAPTER ONE: STOCKING YOUR KITCHEN
PART ONE : THE BASICS

Like anything in life, you only get out of something what you put into it. You don't need to be a genius to figure out that this concept applies to food. How your meals turn out, how they taste and how good they are for you are all directly linked to the quality of the ingredients you use. ☺ As a general rule, always choose fresh ingredients over frozen, and frozen over canned, particularly when it comes to veggies. Dried foods are frequently the exception. You don't often have a choice when buying dried peas, beans or lentils. Some recipes actually call for such things as sun-dried tomatoes or dried fruits. ☺ Okay, let's talk about food.

STAPLES

Staples are those things we cook with and eat on a regular basis. Keep your kitchen stocked with the basic things you'll use most often. You know... stuff like rice, pasta, onions, garlic, sugar, etc. Fortunately, most of these things are cheap and have a long shelf life. Of course, what you consider to be a staple is going to depend on your diet. I'm going to give you a primary list of things that you really should have in the cupboard, even if you don't always use them very often.

Rice, potatoes and pasta: These starchy carbohydrates, along with bread, are some of the most basic of all foods. For a long time they got a bum rap, and were accused of being fattening. Not so. In fact, carbos have the effect of giving you lots of energy and making your body burn calories more rapidly. It's not the potato that makes you fat; it's the butter and sour cream. Higher fibre carbs, like brown rice and fibre-enriched pasta, are even better. Okay, enough already. I'm starting to sound like my parents.

When cooking these starchy foods remember that they love water. They just keep soaking it up until they turn to mush and disintegrate. Don't over-cook them.

RICE

Rice is the staple food for well over half of the people on Earth. It must have something going for it, so I use rice a lot. It's cheap, easy to prepare and makes a good accompaniment to a wide variety of dishes. It's excellent with meals that have a tomato-based, sweetish or spicy sauce.

Just to complicate things a little bit, there are a number of different types of rice. The most common type is polished white rice. It comes in long and short-grain varieties, the latter cooking up a bit softer. You can also get "parboiled" rice, which has been processed to remove most of the surface starch. This keeps the rice from sticking together. This rice can come in handy when making dishes that have a variety of other solid ingredients that must be mixed in. Typically, one cup of raw rice will produce about 3½ cups of cooked.

Brown rice comes from the same plant as white, but it still has the bran husk on the grain. This makes it more nutritious but it takes longer to cook and has a tougher, nutty texture. There's also wild rice, which comes from a different plant altogether and is actually a grass (it should be well rinsed and takes twice as much water and cooking time as regular rice).

The simplest way to make plain rice is by boiling. It's a very easy process if you just watch the time.

TO MAKE ENOUGH RICE TO SERVE 4 PEOPLE (3 ½ CUPS) :

3 cups	cold water
1 tbsp	butter or margarine
1½ cups	white or brown rice (not parboiled)

Bring the water to a boil. Add the butter and allow it to melt. Add the rice and stir. When the water returns to the boil, stir the rice again, cover the pot, reduce the heat to low and allow the rice to simmer for 20 minutes. Check the rice at the 15-minute mark to make sure it's not drying out too quickly. Pay attention to the time; there is a fine line between rice that's done and rice that's burned. When it's tender, remove from the heat and allow it to sit covered in the pot for about 5 minutes.

Most of the pre-processed rice on the market has specific cooking instructions on the package. If you feel inclined to use this type of rice, just follow the directions.

POTATOES

Potatoes are an excellent addition to many meals, particularly anything with gravy. They're cheap and always available. Look for firm ones that aren't cracked, discoloured or sprouting. Store them in a cool, dark and dry container. Russet or Idaho potatoes are good for baking. "New" potatoes (red or white) have very thin, almost translucent skin. They're very moist and are good for boiling. Serve them cold in a salad or hot with a little butter, salt and pepper. The "all-purpose" potato is just what its name implies. Of course, we can't forget my personal fave, the Yukon Gold. This great Canadian potato has a nice pale yellow colour and whips up deliciously creamy when mashed.

Aside from a variety of more complicated, casserole-like recipes, there are three basic ways of cooking and serving potatoes: baked, boiled and mashed.

BAKED

Allow 1 medium-sized (baseball size) potato per person.

Preheat oven to 425°F. Scrub potatoes to remove the dirt. Place potatoes slightly apart from each other on the oven rack. Bake for about 50 minutes for medium-sized potatoes. Cook about 10 minutes more for large potatoes and 10 less for small ones. Test for doneness by stabbing with a fork, which should slide in easily. Serve hot with a little salt, butter or sour cream.

BOILED

Serves four people

4 cups	of water
½ tsp	of salt
4	medium to large potatoes, peeled and quartered

(If you're using "new potatoes" you don't have to peel them)

Measure the water into a large pot and add the salt. Bring to a boil. Add the peeled and quartered potatoes. When the water returns to the boil, reduce the heat to low, cover the pot and cook for about 20 minutes. Test with a fork. They should be firm yet breakable. It may take a few minutes more, but make sure you don't over-cook them. They can get mushy quite quickly. When done, drain and serve.

MASHED

Follow the directions above for boiled potatoes. After draining boiled potatoes, mash them in the pot with a potato masher. Add the following ingredients:

1 or 2 tbsp of butter or margarine
2 to 3 oz   of milk
(or cream if you're feeling decadent)
¼ tsp   salt
(optional- I let people add their own)

After adding the above ingredients, mash the heck out of them until they're creamy and free of lumps.

For a nice twist try adding about ¼ cup of grated Parmesan cheese to the potatoes when you mash them. Presto... Italian mashed potatoes!

PASTA

I love pasta and always keep several kinds on hand. It's good for you and has many uses. There are so many kinds of pasta that it may seem confusing. There are two basic ways of classifying pasta: first, by composition, and second, by shape. Pasta is usually made of wheat (durum semolina). This is the basic pasta we all know and love. There also are egg noodles and oriental rice noodles. Becoming more and more popular these days are pastas made with vegetables. Green pasta is made by adding spinach to the dough, and orange-red pasta by adding tomatoes and other veggies. Others are made with herbs, mushrooms and even squid ink... no kiddin'!

Pasta also comes in a bewildering array of shapes and sizes. With the exception of things like lasagne (broad and flat) or cannelloni and manicotti (pasta tubes) that have specific uses, you can pretty much substitute any kind you want. For the most part I use the dried pasta that's available in any grocery store. It has a shelf life of about a million years and is dirt-cheap. Fresh pasta, available at specialty shops, is delicious but must be kept refrigerated and used within a few days.

Directions for cooking pasta are usually found on the box or bag it came in. If not, use the following method.

4 SERVINGS

3 quarts of water
2 tsp   of salt
3 cups   or ¾ pound of raw pasta

Use a pot big enough to hold the water and pasta with plenty of room to spare so it won't boil over. Bring the water to a boil, add the salt and gradually add your pasta. Maintain a low boil and stir the pasta after it softens up a little to help keep it from sticking together. The thinner the pasta, the less time it takes to cook. Vermicelli takes about 4 to 5 minutes, macaroni and spaghetti about 6 to 7. Lasagne takes the longest at 12 minutes. Prepackaged pasta should have the times on the side of the package. If not, judge for yourself by scooping up a piece and biting into it. Fresh pasta cooks in about half the time. Remember that pasta will continue to soak up water as long as it's in the pot. Use it as soon as it's done.

EGGS

I can't imagine a kitchen without eggs. They're amazingly useful little things. And they're not just for breakfast any more! They have a zillion uses: baking, sauces, thickening, glazing... oh yeah... and eating. You can have them with bacon for breakfast, make eggs benedict for brunch or have a meal-sized omelette or quiche for supper. And let's just set the record straight once and for all: real men will eat anything they damn well please!

When buying eggs always get grade A large. Recipes tend to assume that's what you're using. This is very important when baking or making a sauce because of the chemistry that has to take place. It doesn't matter if you get brown or white-shelled eggs. Just like us, they're all the same inside.

Keep a close eye on freshness. Keep them refrigerated. Note the 'best before' date on the carton and remember: when in doubt, throw them out. One way to test freshness is to put the egg into a bowl of cold water. The bad eggs will float. Kinda sounds like a witch-hunt, eh?

Not only do eggs have to be refrigerated, but so do products containing eggs (especially raw or partially cooked eggs), such as hollandaise sauce or mayonnaise. You should also be aware that eggs could also be contaminated with salmonella, just like the poultry from which they come (or is that the other way around?). The chances of getting salmonella poisoning are slim, but realize there is a risk in eating raw eggs and their products.

FLOUR

For such a seemingly simple thing, flour sure is complicated. It can be made from a host of different grains (wheat, rye, oats, rice, potato, etc.) and can use various parts of the grain (whole wheat, wheat germ, bran, etc.). For the most part, cooks use all-purpose wheat flour. This is the fine powdery white stuff found in your mother's kitchen. While not as healthy as less processed or whole-grain flours, it certainly comes in handy for thickening sauces and gravies and making pastries for things like chicken pot pie.

Store flour in a sealed container in a dry place. Kept like this it'll last longer than you will.

STARCH

Starch is an ultra-fine white powder primarily used as a thickener for glazes and sauces. Corn and tapioca starches are the most common types and they're pretty much interchangeable.

SUGAR

Sugar is one of those ingredients that have consistently got a bad rap. You know... fattening, empty calories. But, unless you have a certain dietary or health problem, sugar in moderation is just fine. Consider your morning coffee. If you use a teaspoon of sugar and one ounce of cream you're getting about 15 calories from the sugar and 40 from the cream. I always have to laugh at those people who take double cream and then use a sugar substitute. Wake up and smell the...

Most of the sugar we use comes from sugar cane and is refined to some degree.

The less refined it is the darker the colour and the more molasses-like the flavour will be. Be aware of the flavour of various types of sugar when using them as a sweetener in recipes. There are times when the molasses flavour would be intrusive. Generally speaking, stick to the type of sugar called for in the recipe.

BUTTER AND MARGARINE

For flavour and richness, nothing can beat cooking with real butter. You can buy it either salted or unsalted. For the most part what you use comes down to personal preference. In some recipes you may see unsalted or sweet butter specifically called for, to avoid an excessively salty flavour. As always, follow the directions.

For frying, the problem with butter is that it will burn at a lower temperature than other fats. You can decrease this effect by mixing it with an equal amount of vegetable oil. You can also use clarified butter, which has the milk solids removed. To clarify butter, place the butter in a heat-proof glass measuring cup or bowl and put it in the oven at 225 °F until the solids settle to the bottom. Carefully pour the clear butter into another container. Keep butter refrigerated.

Margarine is made from vegetable fat and is used as a substitute for butter. For the cook, the problem with margarine is the inconsistency in how it's made and what happens to it when it's heated. In fact, "light" margarine often contains water. Better just stick to butter or oil. If you do use it, keep it in the fridge.

OIL

While not as rich as butter, vegetable oils are certainly cheaper, easier to work with and don't burn as easily. There are many different types of oil from which to choose: corn, peanut, sunflower, safflower, etc. Most oils are so highly processed that they lack their own distinctive flavours or aromas. Sesame seed oil has a very distinctive and strong aroma and flavour that is characteristic of Oriental cuisine. It is used more as a flavour enhancer than a frying medium and is used in small amounts. I wouldn't recommend using it unless called for in a recipe or you're experimenting with a Chinese-style stir-fry or something like that.

If health concerns you, as it does me, oils like canola and olive are commonly considered to be the best for you. Both are low in saturated fats and that nasty old cholesterol. Both oils have their uses. Canola is cheaper but has little flavour. Use it if adding flavour isn't important.

Olive oil is more expensive but adds a wonderful richness to food. There are many different types. They come from various Mediterranean countries such as Italy, Greece and Spain. Like wine, the flavour is greatly affected by the soil in which the olives are grown. A general rule is that the darker the colour, the stronger the flavour. It should be "virgin" or "extra virgin," meaning that the oil was obtained in the first cold pressing of the olives and, therefore, is of higher quality. Store it in a cool, dark place.

VINEGAR is something I always keep on hand but don't use a lot. That's okay, it's cheap and lasts forever. You also don't need to use much because of the potency of flavour. Keep in mind the acidity of vinegar. Store vinegar in glass or plastic containers. Use glass bowls to hold vinegar-based marinades.

There are four basic types of vinegar: distilled white, cider, malt and wine (red or white). These vinegars all have different flavours and are not generally interchangeable. You can also get rice vinegar, which may be called for in Oriental recipes. Balsamic vinegar, though still pretty tart, is a sweetish tasting vinegar from Italy. It's delicious mixed with olive oil on salads and on bread as a substitute for butter. Herb vinegar is usually made with wine vinegar and is flavoured with various combinations of herbs. These specialty vinegars are most commonly used in salad dressings.

SALT

What really needs to be said about something as simple and basic as salt? Surprisingly enough, it's a complex ingredient that's full of controversy. It's one of those things that you literally can't live without. Yet too much salt can lead to a host of health problems like hypertension and kidney trouble. Most of us in North America grew up getting way too much salt in our diet. It was a result of our prepackaged, over-processed dietary habits and our lack of experience with other seasonings like herbs and spices.

Salt also has some unfortunate side effects. It tends to draw out the natural juices of those things being cooked. This isn't so much of a problem when creating soups or stews because a blended flavour is the desired effect. But when you're grilling, roasting, boiling or frying meats and veggies, salt tends to dry out the food through osmosis (remember your basic biology?). To avoid this problem, add the salt near the end of the cooking process.

That's not to say salt doesn't have its uses. When used properly it can help add a little zing to foods without masking natural flavours. It also helps vegetables to keep their colour when boiled.

Ordinary table salt is fine for most kitchen tasks. Store it in a dry place. To keep salt from sticking together in the salt shaker, add a dozen grains of uncooked rice. This helps absorb the moisture that causes salt to stick.

BOUILLON

I doubt if you'll find a cook anywhere who will claim that any commercially made stock or dried bouillon cube is as good as real home-made stock, lovingly prepared in the best time-honoured tradition. Having said that, I must confess that I use the commercial stuff almost exclusively. Why? Because I'm lazy and seldom have the time or desire to make something that's really only an ingredient for making something else. The process involves browning various meats and then simmering them for several hours with various herbs and vegetables.

There are countless stock recipes available and should you get the urge, you can consult a basic cookbook like Fannie Farmer or Joy of Cooking to get one that turns your crank.

I find that a good quality commercial stock works okay for me. In fact, you'd be surprised how many excellent and high priced restaurants use them. Stocks are generally available in chicken or beef flavour. You can also find vegetable and fish stock if you look for it. Bear in mind that you tend to get what you pay for. Check out the gourmet section of your grocery store. It can make quite a difference.

One important thing to keep in mind in using commercial stocks is that they usually have a very high salt content. When using them you don't need to add any salt to your recipe.

LEMON JUICE

Lemon juice comes in handy in a wide· range of recipes. Of course, fresh juice is preferable, but lemons don't keep well. Buy one of those plastic lemon juicers and keep it in the fridge. If you're making something extra special, you can always run out and get some fresh lemons. Another use for lemons is to help keep raw vegetables fresher. Some fruits and veggies turn brown or wilt quickly after they've been peeled (notably potatoes and apples). A sprinkling of lemon juice will help prevent this. You can also cover the veggies in a mixture of water and a tablespoon of lemon juice.

WORCESTERSHIRE SAUCE

I wasn't sure if I should include this as a staple. It's hardly one of the basic foods found in our kitchens. Yet it's something I use frequently and wouldn't want to run out of. It adds a delicious... je ne sais quoi to many recipes.

What is it? It's a thin, dark brown sauce containing malt vinegar, tamarind, molasses and a host of herbs and spices. It was brought back to Britain from India during the colonial days of the 19th century. It's quite potent so a few dashes are all you need. It won't spoil so you can just keep it in the cupboard. Oh yeah... it's pronounced "wuster-sher" or sometimes even just "wuster."

SOY SAUCE

Made from soybeans, roasted wheat, yeast, salt and sugar, soy sauce is a staple in Oriental cooking. It's indispensable in a stir-fry and I always keep it on hand. It's widely available, cheap and has a long shelf life. If you have an Oriental food store nearby, do yourself a flavour and buy a good quality soy sauce.

If you really enjoy Oriental cooking, there are a host of different sauces that are delicious and fun to experiment with: oyster, hoisin, black bean, teriyaki, etc. They can be great additions to stir-fries, marinades, barbecue sauces and anything else your imagination can come up with. Go nuts.

HERBS AND SPICES

I grew up in a small town. We were middle-class WASPs. Dad went to work, Mom stayed home and the five kids were all boomers. You know the story. Not too exciting. Food pretty much followed the same path. Dad was basically a meat and potatoes man. The most adventurous it got was spaghetti and meatballs or lasagne. I'm not complaining, mind you. The food was always good and plentiful. It was a classic case of ignorance being bliss. We were products of our heritage. We just didn't know any better.

I spent my first year after high school travelling in Europe and Asia. Fortunately my folks taught me not to say I didn't like something if I hadn't tried it. Today I can honestly say that there aren't many foods I've tried that I don't like (salt-cod fishcakes spring to mind!).

To me, herbs and spices are more than just an addition to a meal. They are an integral part of cooking. I can't imagine doing without them.

Creating a list of staple herbs and spices is rather difficult. It really depends on personal taste and availability. If you live in a big city you can find just about anything. If, like me, you live in a smaller place you have to make do with what you can find. Fortunately, spicy food is becoming more and more popular. Most grocery stores have all the basic herbs and spices you need for most recipes. In the recipes in this book I've tried to eliminate the need for hard-to-find ingredients.

Generally speaking, herbs are green leafy things and spices are dried seeds, berries or barks (often ground into a powder). Their flavours deteriorate over time so don't buy them in huge quantities. Store them in a dark and dry place. Keep them well sealed to maintain freshness and prevent the aromas and tastes from mingling in the spice cupboard.

Add dried herbs and spices to your dish early in the cooking process. They need time to release their flavours into the food. Most spices can also benefit from a quick sauté (about a minute) in oil to really develop their flavours. Keep stirring them and don't let them burn.

Fresh herbs are great, but they tend to be expensive. They'll keep for a few days if you put the ends of the little stalks or stems into a glass of water in the fridge. They should be added later in the cooking process because their freshness allows the flavours to be released quickly. If you're really into it, you can grow many herbs in your own backyard, flowerpots or window boxes. Just make sure you keep them out of sight if they're the kind you roll up and smoke!

BASIC HERBS AND SPICES

The following is not a comprehensive list. There are dozens of other herbs and spices. As you get into cooking more and more, you'll make your own discoveries and gradually expand your collection.

At first it may seem like a daunting list, but don't think you have to run out and buy them all at once. Acquire them as you need them. Pretty soon you'll discover you have quite a collection.

ALLSPICE Similar in flavour to cloves. Used in baking, but also good with red meats.

BASIL This herb is a staple of French and Italian cooking, arguably the best cooks in the western world. If it's good enough for them it's good enough for me. It's called for in an incredible variety of recipes. Basil is especially good in tomato-based dishes.

BAY LEAF A pungent herb common in French and Italian foods.

CARAWAY Strong-tasting seeds popular in German and East European cooking.

CINNAMON This tends to be a dessert-oriented spice. It doesn't get much use outside of cakes and sweets, but it can be an interesting addition to some pork- or sausage-based dishes, especially with apples or other fruit. It's also an ingredient in many spice blends such as curry powder, Chinese five-spice powder and Indian garam masala. Cinnamon is sold whole (sticks) or ground.

CLOVES In their whole form they look like tiny little flower buds. That's appropriate because that's what they are! Though usually associated with desserts, whole or ground cloves give a warm and spicy flavour to a variety of recipes. They can be delicious in a soup, stew or casserole, especially when it's cold and miserable outside.

CORIANDER Also called cilantro or Chinese parsley. The seeds (coriander) have a lemony, herbal quality. The leaves (cilantro) are very pungent and are common in Indian, Mexican and Chinese food.

CUMIN Cumin seeds have a sharp, warm flavour. It's been used for aeons in Indian, North African and Arab dishes. It also found its way into Spain with the Moors.

CURRY POWDER Curry is a blend of spices that vary by region, yet it maintains a flavour and aroma that isn't likely to be confused with anything else. You either love it or hate it. Curries are popular in Indian, Thai, Sri Lankan, Caribbean and even Chinese foods. The common form of curry powder is Indian-style. Try to use a good quality curry from the gourmet section of grocery stores or Indian food shops. If it comes from India or Great Britain, it should be good.

DILL Best known in pickling, but also great with seafood and veggies. Be careful because dill can overpower.

GARLIC Most of us have a love/hate relationship with garlic. We love the flavour it adds to so many of our favourite dishes, yet we hate the effects it has on our breath. Me? I say, "to hell with it!" I love garlic and am not about to give it up. I just try to make sure that the people I'm with eat it too, and then no one's at a disadvantage. (Eating some parsley can help reduce the effect of garlic breath.)

Garlic bulbs are covered in a white, onion-like skin. Peel the skin back and you find a cluster of cloves that resemble large almonds. These also have a skin, and once peeled they have a glossy sheen and are firm to the touch. The clove is the basic garlic unit used in cooking. Garlic powder is okay if you're in a hurry, but try to use

fresh if at all possible. If using the powder, 1/8 of a teaspoon equals about one small clove. Don't use "garlic salt" in any recipe. It's okay for sprinkling over a steak, but it's not a substitute for the real thing.

When buying garlic, look for firm bulbs without any sprouts. Store it in a dark and dry place, not in a sealed container or the refrigerator.

Like onions, raw garlic has a very strong taste and smell (now that's an understatement!). The flavour and odour of garlic are released when it's chopped. The finer it's chopped, the stronger it is. Cooking makes the effects of garlic subtler. Never allow garlic to brown when frying or sautéing because it becomes quite bitter.

GINGER Often used in desserts, dried ground or freshly grated ginger is also excellent in chicken or fish recipes and is a staple of Oriental, Caribbean and Indian style cooking.

MARJORAM A strong-tasting herb, marjoram is good with fish and poultry and is popular in Mediterranean cuisine, particularly Greek.

MUSTARD When we think of mustard, we usually picture the old stand-by condiment for hot dogs and hamburgers. At the risk of sounding like a snob, this is mustard in its worst form. Mustard seeds vary in colour from mustardy yellow (appropriate, eh?) to a dark brown. They're normally ground and, often, blended with water, vinegar, wine and other herbs or spices. The most common mustard powder available in grocery

stores is dry English mustard. You can use this in recipes calling for dry mustard. It's deceptively strong, so go easy.

Prepared mustards have recently overrun our grocery store shelves: Dijon, Bordeaux, Provençal, Sweet-German or whole-grain country-style… the list goes on. You can even cook with them in sauces, marinades, etc.

NUTMEG This multipurpose spice is often used for desserts and baking, yet it can add a warm, aromatic flavour to veal, lamb and many vegetable dishes. Its sister spice, mace, comes from the same plant. The lacy covering over a nutmeg seed, mace has a similar taste to nutmeg but is slightly more bitter. For you trivia hounds, these are the only two spices that come from the same plant.

OREGANO This may be the most well known of all herbs and is a staple of Mediterranean cooking. It has a very distinctive flavour and must be used with a little care because it can quickly take over the taste of a dish.

PARSLEY I don't use parsley that often, not because I don't like it, but because of its inconvenience. The dried stuff is pretty tasteless, and bunches of the fresh herb (available in the produce section of the grocery store) usually go mostly to waste. Despite that, it is very cheap and is a good opportunity to use a fresh herb. Raw, it has a spicy, almost medicinal taste. When cooked, it becomes subtle and is good with seafood, soups and stews. Of course you can always garnish with it and chew it to freshen your breath.

THE PEPPERS There are two basic types of peppers used as spice. The peppercorn berry produces common black pepper. The green berry is dried and becomes black. It's probably the most common spice we use in North America and is the only one of the various peppers that I would call an absolute staple. It's readily available in its ground form or as whole peppercorns. Shell out the 10 bucks or so for a pepper mill and use the peppercorns. The flavour is much better. It's one of the few times you'll have easy access to whole spice.

Green peppercorns are also unripe berries, but they're freeze-dried or packed in brine or vinegar, thus preserving their colour. White pepper comes from ripe berries, but lacks the flavour of green or black. Hey, did you know peppercorns were once so valuable they could be used as currency and were literally worth their weight in gold? (Just a little "Cliffy" type of info for ya!)

There are also a variety of chili peppers (jalapeño, cayenne, etc.) that may be used fresh, dried or ground to produce the fiery hot flavours in Mexican, Indian and Oriental cuisine. The rule of thumb with these little suckers is the smaller they are the hotter they are. There are also many chili products on the market. Common chili powder (for dishes like chili con carne) is a mixture of ground chilies and a variety of other herbs and spices. Paprika is a red chili powder usually associated with Central European food. It's available in two types: hot and sweet. Chili sauces like Tobasco and Louisiana-style hot sauce are made from chilies, vinegar and sometimes other herbs and spices. Chili pastes are common ingredients in Indian and Oriental recipes.

These chili products aren't what I'd call staples but are good to have around. Buy them if you decide to make a dish that calls for them and then keep the remainder on hand for future use.

Caution! Always take care when using chilies or their products. Keep your fingers away from your eyes and always wash your hands after handling them.

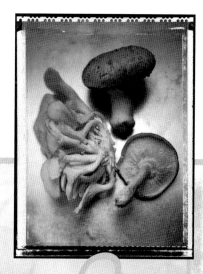

ROSEMARY This distinctive and aromatic herb is delicious with poultry, pork and lamb. It's used in a wide variety of European and North American recipes. A little caution is called for because the flavour can quickly overwhelm.

SAGE A strong herb, good with strong-tasting meats like pork, beef and game and as an ingredient in sausages.

TARRAGON This herb has a subtle lemony flavour and is excellent with chicken, fish and even game. It is a common ingredient in French cuisine, a main component in "fines herbes" and the flavouring for béarnaise sauce.

THYME Like basil, thyme is one of the most basic herbs. Oddly enough I never used it much until I visited France. Now I use it tout le temp. It's particularly good with poultry and fish.

TURMERIC Turmeric is a golden-coloured, musky-tasting spice that is often thought of as the poor man's saffron. In cooking it serves a similar purpose, but lacks the richness and delicacy of saffron. It's good in vegetable stews, rice, bean and lentil dishes. It's widely used in Indian cooking.

herbs spices

FRUITS AND VEGETABLES

At one time we were quite limited in the variety and quality of the fresh fruits and veggies we could get at our local grocery stores, especially in smaller towns. Today, because of improved growing techniques and transportation and storage, there's a bewildering array of produce on the market year round. I'm not going to bore you with a blow-by-blow description of each one. But there are some general rules and considerations that will benefit you.

Always prefer fresh produce to frozen and frozen to canned. This is a general rule throughout cooking, but one that may be a bit of a problem for the single person or couple that don't always eat at home because of a hectic lifestyle. The best way around this problem is to buy a limited supply of the more perishable veggies and select recipes that will use them as soon as possible. The more perishable fruits and veggies include those things that don't have as much of a natural barrier to moisture loss, like broccoli, lettuce and spinach.

More durable veggies don't present as much of a problem. These include things that have tough, thick skins like potatoes, onions, carrots, zucchini, etc. These will last well from a week (zuccs, cucumbers and peppers) to several weeks (potatoes, onions, and carrots).

When buying fresh produce, look for firmness, crispness, colour and good weight for size.

Keep most veggies and fruit in a plastic bag in the fridge. Wrap the more perishable ones (broccoli, lettuce, spinach and other leafy greens) in paper towel and then in a plastic bag in the fridge.

Store things like potatoes, sweet potatoes and onions in a cool, dark, dry place.

Frozen veggies are okay in some cases, like corn kernels, peas and spinach (when used as a cooked ingredient in a recipe). With the exception of tomato sauce or paste and some precooked beans like chickpeas and black beans try to stay away from cans. The technology behind canning has long been made obsolete. Most canned goods are mushy and tasteless. Why bother.

At this point, I have to make special mention of one vegetable. I debated where to include this info. It's one of the most basic of kitchen ingredients. But, it is undeniably a vegetable. This very special ingredient is the onion. Onions have the qualities of both a veggie and a herb. They're used in an incredible array of recipes and the bottom line is the onion is a kitchen staple. They add wonderful flavour and can be as strong or subtle as you want. Best of all, they're cheap.

Onions come in a many forms: Spanish, white, red, pearl, shallots, leeks, etc. The most common is the golden-skinned variety sold in the 2- or 3-pound mesh bags in almost every grocery store in North America. Except for the most specialized of recipes, you can always use this type of onion.

Store onions in a cool, dark and dry place. To help keep from shedding too many tears when cutting them, chill them in the fridge for a half-hour beforehand. You can also cut them under cold, running water. If you're using raw onions, cut them and then soak them in cold water for 15 minutes to help neutralize the harsh, acidic taste.

GRAINS AND LEGUMES

Whole grains and legumes (peas, beans, barley, etc.) should be a significant part of our diet. They're excellent low-fat sources of protein, fibre and carbohydrates. Not only that, but they're dirt-cheap and, because they are usually dried, they have a very long shelf life.

The main downside to dried grains and legumes is that they take a fair amount of forethought when making a meal with them. Rice only takes about 20 minutes, but most dried grains and legumes take a significant amount of time in presoaking (often overnight) and cooking (several hours). Don't let that scare you off. Despite the advance preparation, once underway they are very low maintenance. They make excellent ingredients in soups, stews and casseroles. There are also a number of types of beans sold in cans (with or without a flavoured sauce) suitable for use in recipes.

MEAT AND SEAFOOD

Meat and seafood have long been the cornerstone of our western diet. In fact, most of us get way too much animal fat and protein on a regular basis. About 5 or 6 ounces of meat per day is plenty. Having said that, I must admit I am a carnivore. I love a good, thick, juicy steak, Oktoberfest sausages or barbecued chicken. But do yourself a favour: just cut back a little on the amount you eat and improve its quality. Buy low-fat meats and cook them in ways that don't add to the naturally occurring fat.

wine, wine, wine

MEATS AND SEAFOOD (Continued)

Cheaper cuts of meat tend to be tougher. They require long, slow cooking and/or marinating to make them tender. The same is true of poultry. Unfortunately, when you're buying boneless, skinless chicken, it's hard to tell how tough or tender the meat might be. One clue is that larger chicken breasts are typically from older, tougher birds. Of course you can always ask. No! Not the chicken... the butcher!

When buying meat, always check the "best before" date. Fresher is better. Red meat should be... well, uh... red. Shocker. Pork and poultry should be a fleshy, pink colour. Avoid meat that appears dull, brown or dried around the edges.

Fish should actually have a slimy skin. The flesh itself should be moist and glistening and shouldn't have a strong fishy smell. If you're buying whole fish look for bulging, clear eyes, not sunken or cloudy ones (neither one sounds particularly attractive!).

If you have stored meat or fish in the fridge and aren't sure if it's still good, give it the old sniff test. If it smells bad, it probably is. One more health note: never re-freeze previously frozen fish or seafood. It can make you sick. Look for a sticker that says "previously frozen."

Here's a general guide of what types of alcohol go best in what dishes. This guide is based on "conventional" thinking. As always, feel free to experiment.

- **RED WINE** beef, pork, veal, lamb and game.
- **WHITE WINE** poultry, veal, pork, seafood.
- **ROSÉ** poultry, beef, pork, lamb, veal, game, seafood.
- **SWEET FORTIFIED WINES** for rich sauces with beef, veal, chicken.
(MARSALA, MADEIRA, SHERRY)
- **BRANDY** sauces or flambé for various meats or fish.
- **SWEET LIQUEURS** sauces, flambé and stir-fries of various meats and seafood.
- **BEER** marinades or stews of beef and other red meats. Also good in batter for fish and fritters.
- **RICE WINE** Oriental-style stir-fries and sauces.

BOOZE

I love cooking with booze. Sometimes I even add it to my recipes! I suspect that alcoholic beverages have been a part of cooking since the first drunken cook accidentally dropped his glass of whatever into his pot. Why? Booze can impart a wide range of flavours to the dishes to which it's added. The effect can be as subtle as a white wine added to a fish sauce or as bold as Marsala wine used with chicken or veal. The addition of the appropriate alcohol can be the difference between a good meal and a great one.

Like many aspects of cooking, there are a few guidelines but not many hard and fast rules. The first rule is this: if you wouldn't drink it, don't cook with it. Never use "cooking" wines. They're poor quality and are often heavily salted. Also, be gentle when using strong-tasting types of booze like liqueurs and fortified wines. Their flavour can quickly overwhelm a dish's other flavours, especially when a sauce reduces.

Booze can be used at various stages in the cooking process. Meats can be marinated to tenderize and add flavour. The addition of booze during the simmering period can create a depth of flavour or richness that is fantastic.

And, of course, who could forget the flambé: an exciting burst of flame just before the meal that's a very simple yet impressive technique. When it's done at the end of the cooking process, the flavour doesn't "blend" with the meal but provides an additional "layer" of taste to the dish. Make sure the liquor or brandy has a high alcohol content (30 to 40%) and is warmed slightly before pouring it into the pan. Apply the flame immediately and watch your hair and eyebrows. Oh yeah, don't forget to save a few glasses for drinking!

CONVERSIONS AND SUBSTITUTIONS

One of the things that can irritate and confuse novice cooks is how to calculate how much of an ingredient you need to use when you have to substitute dry for fresh, or when the cookbook is metric or imperial and you only have American Standard measuring cups or whatever. Here are a couple of helpful lists of measurement-related things that are good to have on hand.

U.S. STANDARD MEASUREMENT EQUIVALENTS (LIQUID):

1 teaspoon	= 1/3 tablespoon
1 tablespoon	= 3 teaspoons
2 tablespoons	= 1 fluid ounce
4 tablespoons	= 1/4 cup
5 1/3 tablespoons	= 1/3 cup
8 tablespoons	= 1/2 cup
16 tablespoons	= 1 cup
1 cup	= 8 ounces
2 cups	= 1 pint
1 quart	= 2 pints
1 gallon	= 4 quarts

LIQUID MEASUREMENT EQUIVALENTS:

U.S. Standard	Imperial	Metric
1 teaspoon	5/6 teaspoon	5 millilitres
1 tablespoon	5/6 tablespoon	15 millilitres
1 cup	5/6 breakfast cup	236 millilitres
1 pint	5/6 pint	473 millilitres
1 quart	5/6 quart	946 millilitres
1 gallon	5/6 gallon	3.785 litres

DRY MEASUREMENTS

Remember that U.S. Standard dry measurements are about 1/6th larger than their liquid counterparts. You can buy measuring cups with both wet and dry markings on them. This comes in very handy at times. When making most of the recipes in this book, precise measurement isn't crucial. Remember that cooking is an art and baking (pastries, pies, cakes, etc.) is a science because chemistry is a factor.

As well, Europeans (using imperial or metric systems) tend to measure dry goods by weight (ounces or grams). Here are a few basic equivalents for some common ingredients.

DRY MEASUREMENTS BY WEIGHT

U.S. Standard	Imperial	Metric
Flour, 1 cup	5 ounces	150 grams
Butter, 1 cup	8 ounces	225 grams
Dried beans, 1 cup	8 ounces	225 grams
Dried pasta, 1 cup	8 ounces	225 grams
Rice (raw), 1 cup	8 ounces	225 grams
Grated cheese, 1 cup	4 ounces	115 grams
Chopped veg, 1 cup	4 ounces	115 grams
Chopped herb, 1/4 cup	1/4 ounce	7 grams

Substitutions, yields and equivalents for some common foods:

Herbs	1 tablespoon, fresh	= 1/2 teaspoon dried
Garlic	1 small clove, fresh	= 1/8 teaspoon powdered
Ginger	1 tablespoon grated, raw	= 1/8 teaspoon powdered
Butter	1 cup	= 1/2 pound
Cheese	1 pound	= 4 to 5 cups grated
Lemon	1	= 2 to 3 tablespoons juice
Lime	1	= 1 1/2 tablespoons juice
Orange	1 medium	= 6 tablespoons juice
Potatoes	1 pound raw	= 2 cups mashed
Beans (dried)		
(navy, lima, etc.)	1 pound raw	= 2 1/3 cups raw
	2 1/3 cups raw	= 6 cups cooked
Sugar	1 pound	= 2 cups
(granulated)		

chapter two

Armed and Dangerous: Basic Kitchen Tools

For the novice cook, a kitchen can be a strange and scary place. It's full of all kinds of things to cut or burn you. Then there are all those unfamiliar objects and cooking terms. You know, all those weird-sounding things like roux, bard and macerate. ⑤ Well, true enough, a kitchen can be a little intimidating. It's definitely a place where you want to keep your wits about you. More than once I've received a minor cut or burn. But I still have all my fingers and haven't yet needed to call 911. ⑤ And sometimes a really well-equipped kitchen can seem like a cross between a science lab and a general store. Don't worry… great cooking can be much simpler than many beginners realize. ⑤ All those tools and techniques can come in handy at times and can also be a lot of fun. But the lion's share of recipes can be made with only a few simple tools and methods. What follows is a list of basic kitchen tools and cooking methods you'll need to get yourself started.

LARGE CAST-IRON SKILLET The skillet is the most important cooking vessel known to man. It's multipurpose and economical, conducts and holds heat well, and lasts forever. It can be used for frying, sautéing, braising, simmering, poaching, etc. Indispensable. Have one about 12 inches or more in diameter.

POTS You should have a couple of good pots of various sizes. Unfortunately, this is definitely one area where the money you spend is directly related to the quality of the thing you buy. Basically, the heavier the pot the better it is. You should have a large soup or stew pot (8 quarts or litres), a couple of mid-size pots (1 to 2 quarts or litres) and a small pot of about 2 cups (handy for sauces and melting butter, etc.). A double boiler is also good but not essential. You can always just put a heat-proof glass mixing bowl over hot water in a small or medium pot. Also have at least one large casserole dish or Dutch oven. One about 4 inches deep that holds about 2 to 3 quarts is a good size. Try to get one that can be used on top of the stove (for gravies and such).

GOOD SHARP KNIVES Using a knife is one of the most basic of all kitchen tasks: cut, slice, dice, mince, score, julienne, chop. You get the idea. A good sharp knife should be respected, not feared. You must pay attention to what you're doing, but a sharp knife eliminates having to use excessive pressure while cutting. It's usually a dull knife that causes injuries.

For most tasks you can easily get away with one multipurpose knife. I have one of those ever-sharp knives with a good, heavy 5 or 6-inch blade. The case has a sharpening device inside that keep it razor-sharp all the time. I paid only 10 or 15 bucks for it and it's served me well for almost eight years. It's also nice to have a bread knife and a large, heavy-bladed knife or cleaver to deal with large cuts of meat or bone. A knife sharpener isn't a bad investment, either. The simplest type to use comes in the form of a plastic or metal handle with a set of interlocking metal disks through which you draw the blade of the knife. The old-style sharpening "steel" takes a little practice to use well. To get a good edge, draw the blade across the sharpener at an angle of no more than 15 degrees. Do each side evenly until a good edge develops.

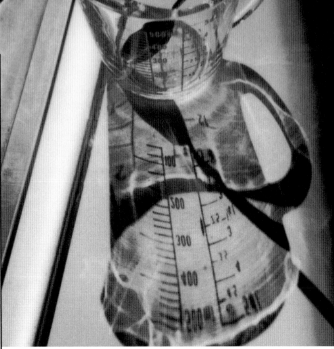

CUTTING BOARD While we're on the topic, a nice heavy cutting board will save a lot of wear and tear on your counters. Ideally, you should have one for meats and one for fruits and veggies. Scrub them well after each use, especially after cutting chicken. You'd hate to invite a date over for supper and have Sam n' Ella crash the party!

TONGS A good pair of spring-loaded chef's tongs is one of the most useful of all kitchen tools. One of the best things about them is that they almost become an extension of your own hand. This gives you great control. You can turn food in a pan, on the barbecue or under the broiler, move hot plates or pans, etc. A professional cook is never very far from his or her tongs. You should be able to pick up a good pair for less than 10 bucks.

PEELER/PARER One of those little knife-like things with a slot on one side for peeling potatoes, carrots, apples, etc. They're not essential but they're dirt-cheap and make the job a lot easier.

BOWLS Have several on hand to perform a variety of tasks like mixing, marinating and holding "prepped" food (a term used to describe raw food that's been cut, peeled or otherwise made ready to cook). It's good to have several sizes but it doesn't really matter what they're made of. (I prefer Pyrex glass.)

MEASURING CUPS One or two Pyrex heat-resistant glass cups with wet and dry measurements marked on them are ideal. They're essential for baking pastries, cakes, etc. Though most cooking doesn't require precise measuring, there are times when it's important. You should also have a set of measuring spoons. Once again, they're more essential for the baker.

MIXING SPOONS A couple of large wooden spoons are perfect for all mixing tasks. One of the nice things about them is that they don't conduct heat. A stout handle is good so you can get a grip while mixing or stirring.

CAN OPENER AND CORKSCREW/ BOTTLE OPENER Pretty obvious, I think.

SPATULA/FLIPPER A sturdy metal flipper for eggs, pancakes, meat, etc. is a basic tool. Try to get one with a wooden or plastic handle that won't heat up.

POTATO MASHER Self-explanatory. You can pick one up cheaply at any department store and most grocery stores.

GRATER Good for cheese and veggies, etc. Once again, cheap and easy to find.

COLANDER One of those basket-like devices for straining things like pasta. It's not essential, but it sure is handy. A good metal one is best, but plastic will do.

WIRE WHISK Perfect for beating liquids, eggs and sauces. A wire area 4 to 5 inches long is good.

SPLATTER SCREEN A round metal mesh screen with a handle that's used to prevent splashing or spattering hot fat or liquid from burning you.

PASTRY BLENDER This device is very useful if you plan to start baking. It's basically a semicircle of metal with slits cut into it attached to a handle. It's designed to mix flour with shortening or butter.

ROLLING PIN Essential for baking. Get a good sturdy wooden one.

BAKING PANS A variety of pans are available for many baking tasks. The shapes and sizes generally conform to common ideas of what baked goods look like. You know… large round ones for cakes, shallow round ones for pies, rectangular ones for loaves and little muffin tins for muffins and cupcakes. Also, cookie trays for you know what. A cooling rack is also a good idea if you're really into the baking thing.

POWER MIXER A nice powerful one is a real arm saver if you plan on baking a lot. One that can handle heavy batters is a good idea. If you really want to go big, get one that'll do bread dough. Not cheap.

PEPPER MILL This device receives honourable mention here because of the benefit of using freshly ground pepper. If you love pepper like I do, you'll soon see what a difference the fresh stuff will make to your recipes. Truly wicked.

Like any pursuit, cooking is full of its own jargon. To the outsider it can sound very complicated and impressive. When it comes right down to it, most of it's really pretty simple and the majority of tasks can be mastered with only a little practice.

There are essentially two ways to serve food: *raw or cooked*. As methods go, you're likely to find the former way easier (ruining a salad is a tough trick to master). I'm not going to devote much time to raw foods here. The most important thing to remember is that raw food demands the best and freshest ingredients you can find. If you start from this premise you won't likely go wrong.

Cooked food is generally the thing that gives people problems. Applying heat to food changes it. When it's not done right, food burns, dries out, overcooks, gets lumpy or soggy or limp… you get the picture. Most of these problems have one basic solution: timing. Getting a meal to turn out properly with all components done at the same time can be tricky. To help you master this problem, I'll make several suggestions.

1. Read the recipe(s) you're using and become familiar with the ingredients and methods used.

2. Gather and "prep" all your ingredients before you start cooking. Wash, peel or cut veggies as required, marinate or cut your meat, sort and blend your spices, etc.

3. Until you become more experienced, stick to the recipes and make note of the time required for each task.

Pay attention to what you're doing and don't try to do too many things at once. Always watch the heat. You might also want to stick to simple one- or two-pot meals that don't require a co-ordination of precise cooking times. Things like spaghetti sauce or curried chicken are ideal for beginner cooks. They can simmer away while you prepare the salad and cook the rice or pasta.

As I said before, cooking involves applying heat to food. That heat can basically be wet, oily or dry. The first category includes boiling, steaming, poaching, braising, etc. The liquid used can be water, broth, wine or a combination of things. Though you might think oily heat is wet, it really has a radically different effect on the way food cooks. Such methods include deep-fat frying, sautéing and other forms of pan-frying. Dry heat includes baking, roasting, grilling, broiling, etc.

The basic considerations in choosing a method are what it does to the flavour, moisture, texture and nutrition of the food. For the most part, the objective is to retain the natural goodness of the food (nutrition and taste) and enhance the flavour by adding herbs, spices or whatever. Sometimes the aim is sort of the opposite. That is, to draw out the taste of the ingredients into a broth or sauce, thus creating a new, blended flavour (such as in soup, sauce or stew).

The key to successful cooking is to choose the right methods to cook the right foods, and then to follow a few simple directions. In many instances, certainly for the new cook, you'll be following a recipe. As you gain experience, you'll begin to notice the effect different cooking methods have on the various foods you prepare. Then you'll be able to start experimenting and trying different things. Though the results won't always be 100% successful, it can be a lot of fun.

Dry heat radiates from a heat source like a fire, coals or a burner element. The main consideration is to ensure that the food is sufficiently cooked through before the outside is overdone or burned. Char-broiling doesn't mean turning your T-bone into a stick of charcoal! On the other hand, a nice golden brown chicken isn't much good if it clucks when you try to carve it. Essentially it comes down to the right amount of heat, from the right source, for the right amount of time. Sound tough? Not really. As I said before, just follow a few simple directions and pay attention to what you're doing. If you're prone to forgetfulness, you might want to use a timer. Many stoves have them on the control panel. If not, just use a cooking timer or a digital alarm clock.

BAKING/ROASTING This is probably the type of dry heat most of us think of first. Heat gets at the food from all sides relatively evenly. Timing and temperature are important factors in successful baking. Stick closely to recipes until you gain some experience. Most recipes will give the time and temp you need to use. After a while you'll get pretty good at judging for yourself.

When baking or roasting meat, there are a couple of general rules that you should follow. First, the meat should be at room temperature before it goes into the oven. Next, preheat the oven to about 450°F and reduce to 325°F after you put the meat in. Cook your meat for 25 to 30 minutes per pound or 40 minutes for pork. Lastly, make sure poultry and pork are always well done (salmonella and trichinosis are both very nasty).

You can test for doneness in a couple of ways. Meat that's firm to the touch is well done. If it feels springy or spongy, it's medium or medium rare. If you're cooking a whole chicken (or other fowl), the leg should turn easily in the socket. If you poke meat with a fork, you can judge doneness by the colour of the juices. The less pink the juice, the more done it is. Remember: pork and poultry juices must be colourless.

One problem with baking or roasting is that food can dry out. Many casserole-type dishes have a fair amount of liquid in them, but they can dry out or burn on the bottom. Check on them once in a while and add a little water if necessary. As I said before, stick closely to cooking times and temperatures.

The drying problem can be especially true of meats that don't have a lot of natural fat in them. This effect can be lessened by:
basting pouring the natural juices or other liquid over the meat periodically during the cooking process.
barding covering a baking meat with a layer of fat (e.g., lard or bacon).
larding similar to barding, this involves actually "sewing" strips of lard into the surface of the meat. This is far too labour-intensive for me, but you do see recipes that call for it from time to time.

BROILING This is cooking under a strong, direct heat source. Only one side is cooked at a time. The food is typically placed 3 or 4 inches from the heat source. Most household ovens have a broil setting of 550°F. You must pay attention when you're broiling because food can burn quickly (it sure can be a good way to test your smoke alarm). This method is good for browning things, or cooking steaks or appetizers, but it's not very good for anything that must be thoroughly cooked.

GRILLING This is similar to broiling except that the heat source is below the food. These days the most common application of this method is barbecuing. Grilling is a tasty way to prepare a variety of foods. You can do anything from burgers and steaks to corn on the cob to filets of salmon or shish kebabs. Once again, you have to take care not to burn the food before it's done. Heat can be controlled by either turning the flame up or down (for gas barbecues) or by raising and lowering the grill. Neither process is what you'd call precise. There's no magic formula for this except paying attention and watching your heat. To reduce the problem of "flame-up" from fat falling onto the coals, partially cook fatty meats by boiling or micro-waving for a few minutes. This releases some of the fat before you put it on the grill. This is especially good for poultry (skin on) or sausages.

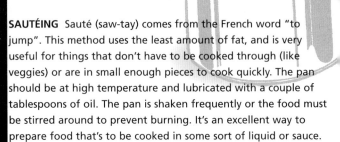

Oily heat includes all the types of frying, with sautéing using the least fat and deep-frying the most. There are a couple of general considerations for these methods. First, what type of fat or oil to use. You can choose from butter, margarine, oil, vegetable shortening or lard. In my opinion, for the vast majority of frying purposes you can use either oil or butter.

Meats tend to have their own natural fat and little oil or butter needs to be added when cooking them. This naturally occurring fat adds a lot of flavour to a meal. Bacon or ham can often be a delicious addition to some recipes. In general, however, I try to find leaner cuts of meat or trim away some of the excess fat, leaving just enough to enhance the flavour. If you find too much fat in the pan, simply drain some away, strain the food through a colander or sop some of it up with a piece of paper towel.

Keep in mind that temperature is the key factor in successful frying. Too hot and the food will burn or, worse, the oil will catch fire. Food cooked in too low a temperature will absorb the excess fat and turn out greasy. For the best results, heat the oil over medium/high heat to the "point-of-fragrance" (when you can smell the oil's fragrance rising from the pan), about 375°F. Make sure the food is about room temperature and is fairly dry to the touch. Excess water or moisture will cause a lot of oil to spatter around. Not pleasant. Also, batter won't stick well to wet food. Don't add too much food to the pan at once because the temp will drop too fast and the food will absorb more fat.

In the unlikely event that fire breaks out, don't panic. If it's a quantity of oil that might spill, don't try to move the pan. Turn off the heat and smother the flames with salt, baking soda or the lid (if you can do it without burning yourself). Never throw water or other liquids into hot oil or to put out a grease fire. Anyway, it's not going to happen if you pay attention. If oil starts to smoke, it's too hot. Reduce the heat.

SAUTÉING Sauté (saw-tay) comes from the French word "to jump". This method uses the least amount of fat, and is very useful for things that don't have to be cooked through (like veggies) or are in small enough pieces to cook quickly. The pan should be at high temperature and lubricated with a couple of tablespoons of oil. The pan is shaken frequently or the food must be stirred around to prevent burning. It's an excellent way to prepare food that's to be cooked in some sort of liquid or sauce.

PAN-FRYING Done in a skillet over medium heat. Use a little more oil than when sautéing. The meat (no more than 1 1/2 inches thick) is often breaded, floured or battered. The idea is to seal in the food's natural juices by cooking on one side until the juices start appearing on top. Flip (the food!) and cook for an equal length of time on the other side.

DEEP-FRYING This is one of the most difficult and potentially dangerous of all cooking methods. Nice upbeat intro, eh? Obviously, it isn't a method that I recommend. First of all, never deep-fry in anything but an electric deep-fryer. The thermostat helps keep the oil at the right temperature, for both cooking and safety reasons. When I was about 16, a neighbour's house burned down because of an oil fire on the stove. One of the firemen said that oil can go from cooking temperature to a raging inferno in about two minutes. He said that people get side-tracked by the TV or the kids for a couple of minutes and come back to find the kitchen in flames. So pay attention.

Cooking temperatures must be precise. This is more difficult than it sounds because the temp changes so much when food is put into and taken out of the oil. Cooking in small batches can help solve this problem.

Wet heat includes a wide variety of methods of cooking food in water, stock and other water-based liquids. Such methods are frequently used in conjunction with others, like first sautéing the meat and veggies and then stewing them in stock, wine and tomato sauce.

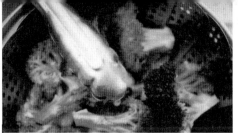

BOILING Boiling is done in water at 212°F (at sea level), that is, the temperature at which bubbles continuously and rapidly break the surface. It's a useful method for some aspects of cooking, but I don't recommend it for general food preparation. It has the tendency of drawing out the food's natural juices. Have you ever seen a piece of boiled meat? Tough and grey. Not very appetizing. It's okay for starchy foods like pasta, rice and potatoes. They draw water into themselves as they cook. Most foods cooked in water (or a similar liquid like stock) are subjected to boiling temperatures for only a few minutes. The heat is usually reduced to a simmer (about 150°F). This is true even of boiled eggs. Excessive boiling amounts to rough treatment. We're aiming for a kinder, gentler kitchen! Remember that the temperature of the water drops when you put the food into it. Add your food gradually.

SIMMERING This is one of the most useful of all methods. At about 150°F the bubbles barely break the surface of the liquid. It treats food more gently than its rough counterpart. It allows food to cook and tenderize without drawing out all the natural goodness. For meats, this is especially true if the food has been sautéed or pan-fried to seal in the juices. Simmering is the method used when making soups, stews, fricassees, pot roasts, braises, etc. Poaching is also akin to simmering. I mention it separately only because it's so often misunderstood. Many people only think of poaching eggs, and even then don't do it right. I hate to harp on this gentleness thing, but it's so true. Keep the temperature fairly low. Use a shallow pan. When doing eggs, this'll help keep them from falling apart. You can poach a variety of other things, but I recommend sticking to fillets or steaks of fish (or meat) that will cook quickly, thus retaining their natural juices. Most poaching is done in only a few minutes. This results in food that's moist and delicious… especially when you add things like white wine, lemon juice, stock, herbs or spices to the water.

DOUBLE-BOILING No, no… this doesn't mean boiling it twice. Essentially, this is cooking in one pot or vessel while it is placed over a pot of boiling or steaming water. There are specific pots for this purpose included in many pot sets. One pot is slightly narrower than the other and has a lip around the middle. It fits partway down into the other pot. You fill the bottom pot partway with water, leaving a gap between the top pot and the water level in the bottom pot (for steam to accumulate). You can also use a metal or heat-resistant glass bowl as the top part. This is an excellent way of cooking things that would be ruined if burned or boiled, especially when you've got a lot on the go or you're prone to memory lapses. It's just the ticket for melting butter or chocolate or making sauces, especially if they contain eggs or cream that might curdle, separate or overcook.

STEAMING A steamer is excellent for cooking veggies and fish. For veggies you can get one of those collapsible metal ones that looks like a radar dish. For fish you need either an oblong steaming basket or something that will raise the fish up above the surface of the water in the pan. Because the steam is hotter than boiling water, this process tends to be very quick. A little caution is necessary because food can go from being done to being mush in a couple of minutes. Maybe that's how they make baby food?

Ideal veggies for steaming include broccoli, cauliflower, green beans, snow peas, corn on the cob, zucchini, carrots and squash. The cooking times for these things vary from 5 to 15 minutes. Timing depends a lot on personal preference. I like most of my veggies to be hot, yet still crisp. Broccoli, zucchini, cauliflower and snow peas cook more quickly than carrots, squash and corn. A rule of thumb is the tougher or more fibrous the vegetable, the longer it takes to cook.

When steaming fish remember that, as with poaching, over-cooking will remove much of the natural juices and flavour. The fish shouldn't be more than about 2 inches thick. If it's too thick, the outside will begin losing its flavour and tenderness before the inside is cooked. About 5 or 6 minutes per pound is usually long enough. Fillets are the simplest to do. My preference is to poach fish, rather than steam it. But steaming is a good, healthy way to cook fish.

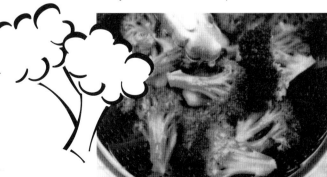

Preparing food prior to cooking involves cutting, mixing, marinating, etc. Knowing what these terms mean may or may not be all that important. But it can help you read and understand a recipe and achieve the effect intended by the recipe's creator.

Beat to mix quickly to make a mixture both smooth and light by beating air into it. Use a fork, wooden spoon, whisk or electric mixer.

Blend to mix two or more ingredients thoroughly. This can be done with wet or dry ingredients and you can use your hands or a tool.

Chop the basic cutting term.

Deglaze after roasting meat in the oven a sticky brown substance remains in the roasting pan. This stuff is essentially browned meat juices and fat and is called "glaze." Thinning the glaze down by stirring in a liquid (stock, wine, etc.) creates a delicious sauce that can be used "as is" or as the basis for a gravy.

Dice to chop into small pieces about the size of a corn kernel or small pea.

Dredge to coat a food in a powdery substance (flour, fine bread crumbs, sugar). This can help seal in juices during cooking.

Drizzle to sprinkle food lightly with a liquid.

Fold to gently mix one fluffy ingredient into another so as not to "unfluff" them. Use a large wooden spoon or a rubber spatula.

Julienne to make thin strips of a veggie. First slice the veg, then cut the slices into strips.

Marinate to cover food in a liquid (usually acidic) prior to cooking so that it tenderizes and soaks up some of the flavour.

Mince to cut very finely; smaller than dicing.

Mix the generic term for combining two or more ingredients. (No kidding!)

Pare to peel.

Reduce to boil down a liquid to reduce volume. (Where do they come up with these technical terms?)

Score to slash meat to tenderize it and help it keep its shape while cooking.

Slice to cut a vegetable across the entire width, so as to make little cross-sections of whatever it is. Slices are generally about 1/8 of an inch wide.

Whip very vigorous beating to lighten and increase volume. Use a whisk or electric beater.

Steppin' Out:
A Few Basic Recipes

SAUCES AND GRAVY

Making a good gravy or sauce is a task that gives a lot of people problems. That's not surprising, since (unlike many of the techniques we've talked about) there's definitely a right and wrong way to do it. It's not that it's particularly hard to do, you just have to do it right. There are two things to consider: *taste and consistency.* Of course taste is important, but it's consistency that gives people a hard time. A lumpy sauce or gravy is something most cooks want to avoid. A wire whisk comes in real handy to make them smooth and silky. There are quite a few ways to thicken a sauce or gravy. I'm going to stick to a few basic ways.

ROUX

This is a fancy-sounding French word ("roo") for one of the easiest ways to thicken a liquid. As well as thickening, a roux adds a delicious richness to a sauce that's hard to beat. It's made by blending equal amounts of melted butter and flour.

To thicken 1 cup of liquid:

2 tbsp   butter
2 tbsp   flour

In a small pot or double boiler melt the butter over low heat. Slowly add the flour while stirring constantly. Continue for 3 to 4 minutes. An advanced technique is to allow the flour to brown a bit to add colour to the sauce. There's a fine line between "browned" and "burned," so if you're going to play around, be careful. I don't have the patience. If you're really keen you can even freeze the roux in tablespoon-sized globs. This saves time in the future.

FLOUR PASTE

Another method that uses flour is to mix it with cold water. While not as rich and a little trickier to do, it's certainly healthier. To thicken 1 cup of liquid begin with the following ingredients:

2 tbsp   flour
4 tbsp   cold water

In a small bowl, gradually add the cold water to the flour, stirring constantly until the mixture is a smooth paste. You can also mix the flour and water in a glass jar: just put the lid on and shake the bejeezus out of them. Stir the paste into the simmering stock or liquid. Allow the sauce to cook for another 4 to 5 minutes to lessen the raw flour taste. Stir often.

STARCH

Starches produce a sauce that's got a glossy, translucent appearance. They're commonly found in Oriental dishes. Oriental cooking usually calls for tapioca starch, which is becoming easier to find. You can always substitute cornstarch, which is readily available in any grocery store. Starch is easy to use because it doesn't tend to get lumpy easily. Follow the same method as with the flour paste described above. One tablespoon of starch will thicken 1 1/2 to 2 cups of liquid.

Mix the following:

1 tbsp   starch
2 tbsp   water or stock

FLAVOURING SAUCES AND GRAVIES

There's no limit to the way a sauce or gravy can be flavoured to enhance any meal. Making sauces and gravies involves adding a base liquid (stock, pan juices, milk, cream, etc.) and flavouring (herbs, spices, cheese, wine, etc.) to one of the thickening agents mentioned above. There are three main things to remember that will ensure your success:

1. Make sure your thickener (roux, starch paste or whatever) is well blended and smooth.
2. Add liquids to the agent gradually, mixing constantly to ensure smoothness.
3. Add other ingredients in the same way; slow and steady, mixing constantly.

This whole process may sound complicated and labour-intensive, but it really isn't as bad as it sounds. It takes less than 10 minutes to make many sauces. Steamed broccoli and cauliflower might sound kind of boring, but topped with a cheddar cheese sauce they become a fancy and delicious side dish to accompany a meal. Fifteen minutes max to do the whole dish. It's a snap if you've got a steak under the broiler or a chicken in the oven. Once you've learned a few basic sauces, you can use your imagination to create your own things. Just remember to consider how the addition of other liquids and ingredients will affect the consistency of the sauce or gravy.

Stir the starchy paste into the hot liquid you want to thicken. I often use starch when I'm in a rush and don't want to risk screwing up.

EGG YOLKS

Egg yolks add a terrific richness to a sauce. They're what make sauces like hollandaise so delicious.

Begin with the following ingredients:

2	egg yolks
1 tbsp	cream

The key to using this method is to make sure the yolks don't cook too much too quickly. Don't add the egg yolks directly to hot liquid. Mix them with about a tablespoon of cream for every 2 yolks. Add a little of the hot liquid to the mixture while beating constantly. Stir this mixture into the rest of the hot liquid. Never allow the liquid to boil after you add the eggs! This task is best performed in a double boiler. Two or three egg yolks will thicken 1 cup of liquid.

BASIC PAN GRAVY

The basis of good gravy is the glaze that forms on the bottom of the pan when meat is roasted or fried. These burned and caramelized bits of meat and fat release delicious, rich flavours when deglazed with a liquid.

Start with these basic ingredients:

1 cup	water
4 tbsp	roux (see recipe above)

Gradually deglaze the roasting or frying pan by scraping away at the bottom of the pan while gradually adding the liquid. In a saucepan make a basic roux. With a wire whisk (or fork), gradually stir the pan liquid into the roux until it becomes thick and smooth. For a basic gravy, use water, but you can use a variety of other liquids: water, milk, wine, stock, etc. Just remember to keep the combined total amount of liquid the same: 4 tablespoons of roux to 1 cup of liquid. You can also season the gravy with some salt and pepper, herbs or spices.

If you don't have pan juices, make a brown sauce by using beef or chicken stock instead of water as a base. Remember that this will not be as rich as the real McCoy. Seasoning can help the finished product.

BASIC WHITE SAUCE OR BÉCHAMEL

Those fancy French words are so cool. Great to toss around when you're trying to impress someone. Anyway, béchamel (bay-sha-mel), which isn't terribly impressive by itself, is used as a base for some of the world's most delicious sauces. This sauce is even easier than making gravy.

4 tbsp	roux (see above recipe)
1 cup	milk

Start with your basic roux. In a saucepan, over low heat and using a whisk, gradually stir 1 cup of milk into the roux. Stir for about 4 to 5 minutes until a smooth thick sauce develops. You can season the sauce by placing a whole small onion (peeled) in the sauce as it cooks. Remove the onion when the sauce is ready to be served. A sprinkling of salt is also a good idea.

Cheese sauce is a very simple variation of béchamel that's a great way to give a little pizzazz to dull steamed veggies. Just gradually stir in 2 to 3 tablespoons of grated cheese (whatever type you prefer) per cup of sauce. Continue to stir until all the cheese is melted and smoothly blended into the sauce.

Mornay sauce is the ultra-classy French cheese sauce.

1/2 cup	water
1/2 cup	white wine
4 tbsp	roux
2 tbsp	grated Parmesan cheese
2 tbsp	grated Gruyère cheese

In a saucepan over low heat, gradually stir the water and wine into the roux. Stir for about 5 minutes until a smooth sauce develops. Slowly stir in the grated Parmesan and Gruyere cheese. To make it richer, add about 2 ounces of cream. Stir until smooth.

VELOUTÉ SAUCE

Hey, more French! Velouté (vel-oot-ay) is the other granddaddy of sauces. It's also a white, creamy sauce but uses a chicken or fish stock as the liquid. Start with your basic roux and stir in 1 cup of broth. Half an onion (peeled but not chopped) can be simmered with the sauce and then removed before serving. There's no limit to the way this basic sauce can be flavoured. Herbs, spices, wine, beer... When you add flavouring to the basic sauce, allow it to simmer for 5 or10 minutes to develop the flavour.

Espanôle sauce (Spanish or brown sauce) is the beef version of velouté. Freshly ground black pepper and a half an onion are used to add flavour. If you want to, you can replace a little of the liquid with an equal amount of tomato juice and add some freshly chopped parsley.

Marchand de Vin (wine merchant) sauce is traditionally made with a beef base.

4 tbsp   roux
½ cup   beef stock
½ cup   red wine
1 tbsp   lemon juice

Begin with the basic roux and stir in the beef stock and red wine. Stir until thickened and then simmer for about 10 minutes. Stir in the lemon juice and serve. To make the sauce even tastier, add 2 tablespoons of minced onion sautéed in butter during the simmering period. You can make a similar sauce for chicken by using white wine and chicken stock.

Hollandaise sauce is a great accompaniment for veggies, fish and, of course, brunch dishes like eggs Benedict. It's always impressive, especially when your guests find out it didn't come out of a package. Fantastic and not nearly as difficult as you might think. To make 1 cup:

¼ lb   of butter.
3   egg yolks
1 tbsp   lemon juice
a pinch   salt and cayenne pepper

Melt the butter in a double boiler. Separate the egg yolks from the egg whites by straining the whites through your fingers. With a wire whisk, beat the egg yolks in a small bowl with the lemon juice until smooth. Gradually beat in some of the melted butter into the egg mixture. When the mixture is smooth, return it to the double boiler, beating constantly. Add a sprinkle of salt and cayenne pepper. Stir until it thickens. If the sauce thickens too much or curdles, put an egg yolk in a bowl and gradually beat the sauce into the egg yolk.

BASIC PASTRY CRUST

Like mastering sauces and gravies, making a good pie crust is another basic technique that all cooks should learn. The most important thing you need to know is this: relax! Making a good pie crust was the most difficult kitchen technique I ever learned. The first couple I made turned out as tough as shoe leather. Maybe it's because of my WASPish upbringing, but I thought that if the crust didn't turn out it was because I didn't work hard enough to get it right. This is definitely the wrong attitude to take in this case. The problem most people have with making a good crust is that they overwork it. Just chill out and don't get frustrated. Here's a basic, foolproof recipe to make an 8-inch pie shell:

1 cup +2 tbsp   all-purpose flour
¼ tsp   salt
1/3 cup   vegetable shortening
2 to 3 tbsp   ice-cold water

Mix the flour and salt in a mixing bowl. Cut in the shortening with a pastry blender or two knives. Blend the ingredients until the shortening is the size of small peas. This is very important because it's the balls of shortening that allow the pastry to be flaky.

Mix in the water (1 tablespoon at a time) with a fork or your hands. After 2 or 3 tablespoons, the pastry should hold together when pressed into a ball. Lightly sprinkle a kitchen counter with a little flour. Dust a rolling pin (or a wine bottle) with flour and roll the dough out so that it's about 2 inches larger than the pan.

Bottom pie crusts should be gently pressed into the pan, trimmed and crimped around the edges and then chilled in the fridge for about 10 minutes. Pie crusts are typically baked at 425°F for about 10 minutes, and then turned down to 350°F for the remainder of the cooking time (which will vary by recipe).

Part Two: A Collection of Recipes that are Pretty Darned Tasty

In my opinion, cooking is about 90% art and 10% science... and not rocket science, either! For the most part, recipes aren't cast in stone. In fact, none of the following recipes are exactly as I originally found them and I seldom make any recipe the same way twice. If there's something you don't like, leave it out. If you think something might be a good addition, go ahead and give it a try.

As you gain experience, you'll begin to develop an intuition that will guide you in making changes to a recipe to suit yourself or in creating your own recipes from scratch. That's when cooking becomes really fun. There's a profound sense of satisfaction in being able to stare into an almost empty fridge, pulling out a few ingredients and then creating a dish that turns out to be delicious.

So go ahead, use your imagination and don't be afraid to get your hands dirty. Above all, have some fun.

Pete's Top Ten Cooking Tips

1. Always pay attention to time and temperature.
2. Read recipes through before starting. Know what you're doing before you start cooking.
3. A meal is only as good as its ingredients: use the best you can.
4. Choose fresh ingredients over frozen, and frozen over canned.
5. Always taste as you go. Let your tongue be your guide.
6. Do as much "prep" work ahead of time as possible.
7. Try to clean as you go as much as possible: a big mess can dampen anyone's enthusiasm for cooking.
8. You learn a lot through trial and error. Experiment when you want to and don't be put off when things don't turn out perfectly.
9. Draw on the experience of others: cookbooks, friends, mom, etc.
10. Have fun. Don't let cooking become a chore.

chapter three

Get Your Motor Runnin':
A Few Breakfast and Brunch Things

Sometimes cold cereal or a peanut butter and jam sandwich just won't cut it.

Yet one thing about breakfast, brunch and lunch holds true for most people:

minimum fuss, maximum satisfaction. A tall order you say? Nah! Most of the

following recipes can be made in 10 minutes. And the fancier ones can be done

in 15 to 20. They're all made with simple ingredients and most of these dishes

are very versatile.

French Omelette

This type of omelette is really fast: only about 2 to 3 minutes. They can be jazzed up in all sorts of ways, but let's start off by learning how to make the plain omelette for one person.

Begin with the following ingredients:

2	large eggs
a splash	cold water (about an ounce)
a pinch	salt and pepper
1 tbsp	butter or oil

To make your omelette, first crack the eggs into a small mixing bowl. Add a splash of water and a pinch of salt and pepper.

Heat an 8-inch skillet over medium-high heat. A non-stick pan is a real bonus, but not essential. Put 1 tablespoon of butter, olive oil or a mixture of the two in the pan. When the butter or oil is hot, add the egg mixture and immediately reduce the heat to medium-low.

Gently shake the pan back and forth to spread the eggs evenly over the surface. Stir the eggs with a fork or spatula. Allow the liquid eggs to run over any exposed surface of the pan. Using the spatula or an egg flipper, gently fold half of the omelette over the other half (remember that the eggs should be moist on top when you fold it). Allow it to firm up for another minute. Then slide the omelette out of the pan and onto a plate. It shouldn't stick, but if it does just run the spatula or flipper under the omelette to release it. Getting the omelette to turn out perfectly takes a little practice. But it's a really simple process.

Omelettes are best when made individually, but you can make a two-person omelette with 4 eggs and then just cut it in half to serve. Any bigger than that and the omelette begins to fall apart. Hey, ya may as well make scrambled eggs!

As I said before, there are lots of ways to make the plain old omelette more exciting and delicious. Use your imagination. Here are a few ideas: add diced ham, shrimp, crabmeat, lobster, tuna, smoked salmon, red or green pepper, tomatoes, onions, mushrooms, grated cheese. To include these ingredients in your omelette, begin by preparing them first. Some ingredients, such as raw seafood, sausage meat and bacon, must be pre-cooked. You may also want to sauté ingredients like onion, peppers and mushrooms.

Once you've got all your ingredients ready, you're off to the races. Begin your omelette the usual way. When it begins to firm up and is almost ready to fold (after about a minute or so), spread the filling evenly over the centre of the omelette. When the egg is cooked, but still moist, fold the omelette and slide it out of the pan onto a plate. If you're adding cheese, allow the omelette to sit in the pan for an extra minute to let the cheese melt.

You can also add things directly to the beaten egg mixture. Try adding a teaspoon of basil, thyme, oregano or a few pinches of all three, a dash of Worcestershire sauce, a tablespoon of sour cream, $1/4$ teaspoon of Dijon mustard or a dash or two of tobasco sauce.

Serve the omelette with toast, rolls, croissants, juice, fresh fruit or a salad. And remember: omelettes aren't just for breakfast any more, they're great any time of the day.

When I was growing up pancakes were always something special that Mom would sometimes make for us on Sunday mornings. Because of that I always considered pancakes to be kind of a treat, especially if they had blueberries in them. But, pancakes from scratch are actually quite simple to make. They're a little time consuming so you probably won't want to make them when you're rushing off to work or class, but they're fantastic on lazy days off.

Serves 4

1/2 cup	milk (room temperature is best)
1	egg
2 tbsp	melted butter
1 cup	flour
1/2 tsp	salt
2 tbsp	sugar
2 tsp	baking powder

Pancakes

Begin by beating together the milk, egg and melted butter in a mixing bowl. In another bowl, mix together the flour, salt, sugar and baking powder. Stir the dry ingredients into the wet. This is the key part: mix the ingredients so that all the flour is moistened, but don't over-beat it. The batter should end up slightly lumpy. If you over-mix the batter, the pancakes will end up rubbery and won't rise. Use the same approach as when making a pastry crust. Just relax and take it easy!

Next, heat a frying pan or skillet over medium heat. Add about a tablespoon of butter to the pan and spread it around. When it begins to bubble, you're ready to cook. Pour about 1/4 cup of batter into the centre of the pan. When small bubbles appear on the top of the pancake, flip it and cook until browned on the other side. Remove finished cakes to a plate in a warm oven. Very simple, eh?

Here are a couple of pointers to make sure everything works out okay.
1. Don't make the pancakes too large or they will be hard to flip.
2. Use the first one to judge the temperature of the pan. If they're browning too fast, just turn the heat down a little.
3. Add a little more butter to the pan as needed to ensure they don't stick.
4. Don't disturb the pancake for the first minute or so of cooking. The crust should be allowed to firm up before it's moved.

Eggs BENEDICT

Eggs Beny is probably the most classic of all brunch dishes. It's surprisingly easy to make, although a little time consuming and labour intensive. But the end result is well worth the wait, especially for a special occasion. Delicious, classy and romantic. Damn the fat and cholesterol: full speed ahead!

To serve 2 people

4	eggs
2	English muffins, split
4	slices of cooked ham
1 cup	hollandaise sauce

The only part of this recipe that'll give you any difficulty whatsoever is the hollandaise sauce. Follow the directions found in the above section on sauces. Once completed, keep the sauce in the double boiler on low heat and stir every minute or two to prevent it from lumping up.

Okay, now the hard part is done. Next, bring to a boil about 3 inches of water in a pan. When the water boils, reduce the heat to low. When it stops bubbling add the eggs. The best way to do this is to crack each egg into a small bowl one at a time and gently slide the egg into the water. Make sure the eggs are well spaced so they don't stick together. Allow them to sit in the water for about 6 to 7 minutes.

While you're waiting for the eggs to cook, split and toast the English muffins. You can also, if you want, lightly sauté the ham, but it's not necessary. It's a good idea to begin putting the eggs Beny together at this point. Put two halves of a muffin on each plate. Cover each half with a slice of ham.

When the eggs are done, remove them from the water with a slotted spoon, drain well and place each egg on a muffin half. Pour a few tablespoons of the hollandaise sauce over each half. Serve immediately. Garnish with slices of fresh fruit and a sprig of parsley and you've got a very impressive meal.

VARIATIONS

This is a great recipe to play around with.
- Use a toasted bagel instead of the English muffin.
- Try melting some cheese over the ham.
- Replace the ham with sliced smoked salmon or sautéed spinach and mushrooms.
- Make Maltese sauce by adding an extra egg yolk and 2 tablespoons of orange juice to the sauce.

Croque Monsieur

Try this fancy version of a grilled cheese sandwich. Man, those French sure have that je ne sais quoi when it comes to cooking! To make one sandwich, follow this simple recipe.

Begin with these ingredients:

2	slices of white sandwich bread
	Dijon mustard
	mayonnaise
	sliced ham
	sliced or grated Gruyère cheese
1	egg
	a splash of cold water
1 tbsp	each of oil and butter

Spread one piece of bread with some Dijon mustard and the other with mayonnaise. Place one or two slices of cooked ham on the Dijon mustard. Cover the ham with grated or thinly sliced Gruyère cheese. Use another type of cheese if you prefer. Then cover the cheese with the other piece of bread (need I say, mayonnaise side down?).

Beat the egg with a little water in a shallow bowl. Next heat the butter and oil in a small pan and make sure they coat the whole surface. When the butter foams up, dip the sandwich into the egg and coat both sides. Place the sandwich in the pan and cook over medium-low heat until golden brown. Flip and cook the other side. Don't cook the sandwich too fast because you want the heat to penetrate and melt the cheese. Serve, close your eyes and imagine yourself sitting in a Parisian café. Excellent with a café au lait or a glass of champagne and orange juice.

chapter 4

The Opening Round Starters

Appetizers aren't something that you're likely to make just for yourself. But if you're having a small dinner party for a few friends or family (or even a party for two, nudge, nudge), an appetizer can be a classy and delicious way to get the evening under way. ☺ If you're making a nice, somewhat special dinner, you don't want to get bogged down making a complicated or time-consuming hors d'oeuvre or starter. The simplest approach is to serve a nicely arranged tray of cheeses, patés, olives, gherkins, veggies and dips. Many people are fine with this. But sometimes you want a little something extra. Here are a few recipes to get you going.

Devilled Eggs

METHOD

Put eggs in a large pot and cover with cold water. Bring to a boil and reduce heat to a simmer. Cook for 15 minutes. Drain and immerse the eggs in cold water to stop the cooking process. Peel the eggs and slice lengthways down the middle. Remove yolks carefully so as not to damage the little egg-white boats.

In a bowl, mash the egg yolks with the mayonnaise, mustard, Worcestershire sauce, cayenne and salt. The end result should be a creamy yet firm paste. With a spoon or a pastry bag, fill each egg half with the egg paste. Sprinkle with paprika and garnish with a small sprig of parsley.

INGREDIENTS

8 eggs
2-3 tbsp mayonnaise
1 tsp Dijon mustard

dash of Worcestershire sauce

a few pinches of cayenne pepper

a pinch or 2 of salt
paprika for garnish

This is a mainstay of many a cook's appetizer repertoire. Creamy, delicious and a real crowd pleaser. This recipe will yield 16 devilled egg halves. That's plenty for 4 people. Adjust the recipe to suit the number of guests you have.

Bruschetta are crispy slices of authentic Italian garlic bread. Unlike their typical North American cousins, traditional bruschetta aren't smothered in butter and cheese. Bruschetta are simpler and much healthier. They make an excellent appetizer or accompaniment to a wide variety of meals.

Bruschetta and Crostini

THE PROCESS IS SIMPLE.

ASSEMBLE THE FOLLOWING INGREDIENTS:

fresh Italian or French bread,
sliced about 1 in thick
several plump garlic cloves
extra virgin olive oil

METHOD

Prepare a couple of pieces for each person. Cutting the bread on the diagonal makes for a fancier looking result, but it's not necessary. Toast, broil or grill every piece until golden brown (both sides). Select very plump and juicy garlic cloves and slice each down the middle. Rub the raw, juicy ends of the cloves over one side of the toasted bread. Drizzle or brush each piece of bread with the olive oil. Serve immediately.

Crostini are essentially bruschetta topped with various ingredients. The traditional version is to top the crostini with diced ripe tomatoes, chopped fresh basil, a pinch of salt and freshly ground black pepper. Pretty simple, eh? You can have a lot of fun altering the basic recipe to suit your own taste.

TRY these ideas, alone or in combination:
· fresh shrimp, sautéed and chopped
· capers
· Parmesan cheese, grated
· anchovies, chopped fine
· black olives, pitted and sliced
· prosciutto ham, sliced thin
· feta cheese, crumbled
· other freshly chopped herbs like thyme, parsley, cilantro, etc.

Note: Use salt very cautiously if you're using one of the saltier-tasting toppings listed above.

The richness of the scallops combines perfectly with the salty bacon to make a wonderful taste sensation. They make a great informal appetizer for a dinner get-together or just as a snack. They're even better when served with a cocktail sauce. I'm including a very simple version for you to try here.

Serves 4

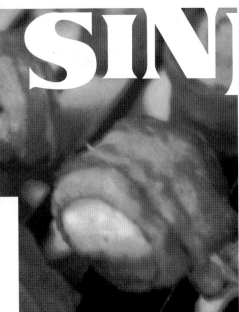

SINFUL scallops

INGREDIENTS		COCKTAIL SAUCE	
8 slices	of bacon, cut in half	³/₄ cup	of tomato ketchup
16	large scallops	2 tbsp	prepared horseradish
	toothpicks, soaked in water	1-2 tbsp	lemon juice
		a few dashes tobasco sauce.	

METHOD

It's a good idea to boil your bacon pieces for about 4 to 5 minutes. This will reduce the amount of fat and help prevent burning and "flame-up." The boiling (as opposed to pre-frying) will allow the bacon to remain supple enough to handle without breaking. Drain and pat dry. Wrap each scallop with a piece of bacon and secure with a toothpick. Broil or grill for about 3 minutes per side.

Meanwhile, combine ketchup, lemon juice, horseradish and tobasco sauce in a small bowl. Mix thoroughly. Arrange scallops on a serving dish and put the sauce for dipping in a serving bowl.

CHICKEN SATAY

INGREDIENTS

about 4 bamboo skewers (soaked in water)	
2 tbsp	shredded coconut
½ cup	hot chicken broth
1 tbsp	vegetable oil
1	onion, minced
1 tbsp	brown sugar
½ tsp	cayenne pepper
3 tbsp	peanut butter
1 tbsp	soy sauce
1	lime
1 lb	boneless, skinless chicken breast (cut into 1-in cubes)

There's something kind of fun about food cooked on a skewer. I guess it's because it's different, a little elaborate looking and you're free to use your fingers. Anyway, it's always a crowd pleaser. Satay comes from Indonesia. The rich peanut sauce is utterly fantastic. It's especially good in the summer with an ice-cold beer.

Starters for 4

METHOD

Let the skewers soak in water while you prepare the satay. Soak shredded coconut in hot chicken broth for about 10 minutes. Strain and reserve stock and coconut. Heat the oil in a small pan over medium heat, and sauté onion for about 2 minutes. Add brown sugar, cayenne pepper and coconut and continue to cook for another minute, stirring constantly. Add the peanut butter and stir for another minute. Mix in the soy sauce and squeeze in the lime juice. The mixture should quickly develop into a thick paste. Stir in about half of the chicken broth. When it boils, cover and reduce to a simmer.

Skewer the chicken cubes evenly onto the bamboo skewers. Don't pack the pieces together tightly. Broil or barbecue for about 3 minutes per side. When they're almost done, check on your peanut sauce. Some of the peanut oil will probably have separated. Give it a good stir to re-combine it. It should be like a thick syrup. If it seems too thick to pour, stir in a little more the chicken broth.

Remove the skewers from the broiler or grill and arrange them on a serving dish. Spoon on the sauce and serve. To go one step farther, garnish with slices of fresh mango, melon, papaya or peaches.

Warm sunshine, cold beer and some shrimps on the barbecue. All the makings of a perfect summer afternoon. The Oriental flavour of teriyaki sauce and ginger are perfect for the shrimp and accompanying vegetables. You can also do this indoors under the broiler. In the winter just turn up the furnace, put on shorts and a T-shirt, grab a beer and pretend it's summer!

Grilled

Shrimp Teriyaki

This can be served as an appetizer or a light main course. If you're in a rush, you can "cheat" by using a ready-made teriyaki sauce available in the Oriental food section of most supermarkets.
Serves 4.

Shrimp

shrimp teriyaki

INGREDIENTS

½ cup	soy sauce
5 tbsp	sugar
1 tbsp	rice wine or dry sherry
1 tbsp	powdered ginger (or 2 tbsp fresh grated)
1	clove garlic, minced (or ¼ tsp garlic powder)
6 - 8	jumbo, tiger or other large shrimp per person, peeled
1	large red and 1 green pepper, cut into bite-sized squares
4	small onions, peeled and quartered
1	zucchini, sliced
4	cherry tomatoes per person

METHOD

Soak 2 bamboo skewers per person in water for at least 10 minutes. Combine the soy sauce, sugar, rice wine, ginger and garlic in a shallow glass dish. Marinate peeled shrimp in the sauce for 20 minutes. Remove shrimp from the sauce and thread alternating pieces of shrimp and veggies onto each skewer. Heat the sauce in a small pot over medium heat until it begins to thicken. Preheat the barbecue or broiler.

Grill or broil the skewers for about 4 minutes per side. Brush occasionally with sauce. Keep a close on eye on things when cooking like this because food can burn quickly when grilled or broiled. The shrimp will cook rapidly and shouldn't be over-cooked, as they become tough. The veggies should be hot, yet crisp.

VARIATIONS

As I mentioned before, this type of dish is open to whatever whim you may have. Teriyaki sauce is excellent with chicken, seafood, pork or beef. Remember that chicken and pork must be thoroughly cooked so don't make the chunks too big. As for the vegetables, choose whatever you want, but remember that this method has a short cooking time at a high temperature. Your veggies will be almost raw on the inside so pick ones that you want to eat that way.

Soups

Soups are wonderful. They're so versatile that they can be served as a starter dish or as a light meal on their own or with sandwiches or whatever. For me they're real comfort food. Great when it's cold and wet outside or when I'm miserable inside!

This is a delicious soup recipe that I created from my memory of a soup I had in Vienna. Though I didn't know exactly what was in the soup, I was able to pick out the main ingredients. I just improvised on the rest and the results were even better than the soup I remembered.

Serves 4 to 6

Serbian BEAN SOUP

INGREDIENTS

1 cup	of white pea beans
2 tbsp	olive oil
1¹/₂ cups	chopped, cooked ham
2	large onions
2	medium carrots, sliced
2	cloves garlic, minced or crushed
1	stalk celery, sliced
1¹/₂ cups	of chopped cabbage
1 tsp	sweet basil
¹/₂ tsp	marjoram
1¹/₂ tbsp	sweet paprika
black pepper to taste	
5 cups	of beef stock
1 tbsp	honey
salt to taste	

METHOD

Soak the dried beans in double the amount of water overnight.

Place the oil in a large pot over medium heat. Sauté ham, onions, carrots, garlic, celery and cabbage for about 5 minutes. Add the basil, marjoram, paprika and black pepper and continue stirring for another minute or two. Add the beef stock, honey and beans and bring to a low boil. Reduce heat and simmer, covered, for about 1¹/₂ hours. Check for the tenderness of the beans and continue cooking until they're done. Taste and add a little salt if needed. Replace lost water as needed. Serve hot with lots of fresh, hearty bread or sandwiches.

SEAFOOD
chowder

My mother had this recipe written on a piece of paper and stuck in an old cookbook. It was stained and frayed around the edges and she can't remember where or when she got it. All she knows for sure is that it's old and it works. Thanks Mom.

Serves 4

METHOD

Heat a large pot or a Dutch oven over low to medium heat. Sauté the bacon, onion, celery and garlic. If not using bacon, use 1 tbsp of olive oil and 1 tbsp of butter. Cook until the onion is translucent and tender but be careful not to burn anything because it will really show in this milk-based soup. Add the coriander and pepper (and salt if you're using it). Stir in the fish stock and wine and bring to a boil. Add the potatoes and cook at a low boil for about 10 minutes. Gradually add the seafood, and when it returns to a low boil, reduce the heat and simmer for another 5 minutes. Check the potatoes: they should be tender but not falling apart. Stir in the milk and heat through, but don't boil the chowder after adding the milk. Taste and adjust the seasoning.

INGREDIENTS

3	slices of bacon, chopped
1	large onion, peeled and chopped
1	stalk of celery, sliced thinly
1	clove of garlic, crushed and minced
1/4 tsp	ground coriander seed
	salt and black pepper to taste
2 cups	fish stock
1/2 cup	white wine (optional)
2 - 3	potatoes, peeled and cubed
1 - 1 1/2	pounds of fresh seafood, cut into bite-size chunks

(Choose a mixture of fish and shellfish: haddock, halibut, salmon, crab, lobster, shrimp, or whatever.)

2 cups	milk (or damn the fat content and use 1 cup of milk and 1 cup of cream)

BOUILLABAISSE

One story about the creation of this amazing fish soup is that it was a gift by the angels to starving religious pilgrims in Provence in southern France. True or not, this dish is definitely akin to a religious experience. I first had this on a warm summer evening in the French city of Arles (of Van Gogh fame). It was perfect with some crusty bread and a bottle of cold rosé. The fish used in southern France is different than what we generally have available here in North America. That's okay, it'll be delicious anyway.

INGREDIENTS

¼ cup	olive oil
1	large onion, finely chopped
4	green onions (white sections only), finely sliced
2	medium-sized tomatoes, chopped
3	cloves garlic, minced
1 tsp	fennel or anise seed (both have a subtle liquorice flavour)

a few pinches of saffron
(You can substitute about ¼ tsp of turmeric if you can't get saffron.)

1	bay leaf
¼ tsp	orange rind, grated

a few pinches celery seed

1 tbsp	parsley, finely chopped

black pepper to taste

½ tsp	salt (omit if using commercial fish stock)
2 cups	fish stock
½ cup	white wine or rosé
½ lb	filet of sole, red snapper, perch, halibut or whatever, cut into bite size pieces
½ lb	jumbo or tiger shrimp, shelled
½ lb	lobster meat, in bite-sized pieces
½ lb	mussels or clams in shell

(Feel free to improvise on the seafood you use.)

METHOD

Heat the olive oil in a large pot or Dutch oven. Add the onion, green onions, tomatoes, garlic, fennel, saffron, bay leaf, orange rind, celery seed, parsley and black pepper. Cook over medium heat until tomatoes begin to break down. Stir in the fish stock and wine. Bring to a boil and then reduce heat and simmer for about 20 minutes.

About 10 minutes before serving, add the fish and seafood and bring to a boil again, then reduce to a simmer. After 10 minutes the clams and mussels should be open and the other fish and seafood done. Serve immediately because if left too long the fish will be overdone and the shrimp tough. Serve with plenty of good bread and a nice cold bottle of rosé, white wine or beer.

French Canadian Split Pea Soup

During a visit to Quebec City a few years back, my girlfriend and I got caught in a nasty rainstorm. We took refuge in a small café and I ordered a bowl of split pea soup. Delicious and soothing. It made being cold and wet a little more bearable. Try this on a lazy Sunday afternoon when you're stuck indoors. It's a simple process to throw everything together and let it simmer away for a couple of hours.   *Makes 4 to 6 servings*

INGREDIENTS

1 tbsp	cooking oil
1 cup	cooked ham, diced
1	large onion, chopped
1	large carrot, grated
1	stalk celery, chopped fine
1	clove garlic, crushed and minced
1/2 tsp	salt
1/4 tsp	black pepper
1 tsp	dry mustard
1	bay leaf
2 cups	dried split peas, rinsed
1 tbsp	Worcestershire sauce
4 - 5	cups water
1/2 cup	of milk

METHOD

In a large Dutch oven or heavy-bottom pot heat the oil and sauté the ham, onion, carrot and celery until onion is tender. Add the garlic, salt, pepper, mustard and bay leaf and cook for another minute or two. Stir in the split peas, Worcestershire sauce and the water and bring to a boil. Reduce to a simmer and cook, covered, for 2 hours. When the peas are soft, stir in the milk and serve. Great with sandwiches or some hearty bread.

Mulligatawny Soup

This delicious chicken soup from India gives you a wonderful warm feeling when you're a little under the weather. I love to make a big pot of this when I get a cold. It has a similar effect to sitting by a fire wrapped in a blanket. Hey, and if you make it spicy enough, it really clears out those sinuses! *Makes 6 large bowls*

INGREDIENTS

2 tbsp	olive oil
1 lb	boneless chicken, chopped into small pieces
1	large onion, chopped
1	stalk celery, chopped
1	large carrot, grated or chopped small
1	medium zucchini, quartered and chopped
1	large clove of garlic, minced or crushed
1	large. apple, peeled and diced without core
1 tbsp	curry powder
1 tsp	ginger powder
2	cloves, crushed
1/4 tsp	cumin
1/4 tsp	coriander
1/4 tsp	basil
4 cups	chicken stock
2 tbsp	Worcestershire sauce
1 tbsp	honey
cooked rice	

METHOD

Add the oil to a large soup pot. Over medium heat sauté chicken until browned. Add garlic, vegetables and apple and sauté for about 5 minutes. Add all dry spices and herbs and cook for another 2 minutes. Stir constantly to prevent sticking and burning (reduce heat if necessary). Add chicken stock, Worcestershire sauce and honey. Add 2 cups of water and bring to a boil. Reduce heat and simmer for about an hour. Replace half of the lost water. Serve the rice separately or add it to the individual bowls as you dish the soup up. Don't add rice or pasta to soup as it cooks because it swells up, becomes limp or just disintegrates!

chapter 5

The Main Event

For the beginner cook, or those of us who don't like much fuss, main courses should be easy to prepare and foolproof. The following recipes are just that: simple, guaranteed and delicious. Many of them are designed to be "one pot" meals for minimum fuss and mess. Most require less than 15 minutes preparation time and are cooked in under half an hour. Those that take longer to cook can be left to simmer or bake while you do your own thing. This feature comes in real handy when you have guests. ⑥ I try to eat healthy most of the time. Lots of fresh fruit and veggies, fish, lean cuts of meat and reduced amounts of fat and salt. Most of these recipes reflect my eating habits. I hope they'll meet your standards. Remember that most recipes can be altered to suit your own habits and taste. You can decrease the amounts of meat, fat, salt or whatever. ⑥ You may find that my serving sizes are on the large side. That's because I like to have enough left over for people to have seconds if they want. That's the best compliment for any cook: guests who sheepishly ask if there's any left in the pot. Actions always speak louder than words. Anyway, have fun with these recipes in the kitchen and at the table.

BABA'S

After I graduated high school, I spent three months travelling in India. I grew to love Indian food and I had quite a few different types of curry. There's an ancient belief that eating curry brings about a sense of well-being. I don't know if there's any scientific basis for this, but I always feel great after a big feed of it. This recipe is an adaptation of one given to me by a friend I made in Bangalore.

Serves 4

METHOD

Chop chicken into bite-sized pieces. Heat half of the oil in a large skillet. Over medium heat, sauté chicken, onion, garlic and carrot for about 5 minutes. Remove from the pan. Heat the remaining oil in the skillet and stir in curry powder, being careful not to burn it. After about 30 seconds add the chopped tomatoes, sweet basil and cumin. Sauté the mixture until it breaks down into a mush (about 5 minutes). Add chicken mixture, chicken stock and honey and simmer over low heat for about 15 minutes. Add the raisins, chopped sweet pepper and apple and cook for another 10 minutes. If you want, thicken with some flour paste or roux. Serve with rice and bread so you can sop up every last drop of delicious sauce.

rriedchicken

INGREDIENTS

1½ lb	boneless, skinless chicken
2 tbsp	oil
1	large onion, chopped
1	clove garlic, minced or crushed
1	medium carrot, grated
1½ tbsp	curry powder
3	large tomatoes, chopped
½ tsp	sweet basil
¼ tsp	cumin
1½ cups	chicken stock
1 tbsp	honey
⅛ cup	seedless raisins
1	medium sweet pepper (red or green) chopped
1	large apple, diced (excluding core)
salt and pepper to taste	

Provençal cooking is deliciously aromatic and uses the herbs and vegetables found in southern France. Whenever you see a dish called "Provençal" you can be sure it contains tomatoes, olive oil, garlic and herbs de Provençe. The last ingredient is one of those imprecise blends of herbs that can be altered to suit your own taste. The herbs most commonly associated with Provençe are thyme, basil, rosemary, savoury, oregano, bay leaves, marjoram, coriander and lavender. If you're an inexperienced cook, try my combo first. As you learn more, feel free to play with the ingredients to suit yourself.

Makes 4 big helpings

chicken PROVENÇAL

INGREDIENTS

1½	pounds boneless, skinless chicken
1	egg, beaten
2 cups	flour or fine bread crumbs
4 tbsp	olive oil
1	large onion, chopped
2	cloves garlic, minced or crushed
8	medium mushrooms, sliced
1	stalk celery, sliced
1	carrot, grated or sliced
3	large tomatoes, chopped
1½ cups	chicken broth
1 cup	white wine
1 tsp	thyme
1 tsp	rosemary
1 tsp	sweet basil
½ tsp	coriander
1	bay leaf
1 tbsp	Worcestershire sauce
1	medium red pepper, cored and sliced
1	small zucchini, sliced

salt and black pepper to taste

METHOD

Dip chicken pieces in beaten egg and coat with flour. Place half of the oil in a large skillet. Brown the chicken on both sides over medium heat. Remove from skillet. Add remaining oil to the pan and sauté onions, garlic, mushrooms, celery and carrot. When onion are lightly golden, add the chopped tomatoes. Cook over medium-low heat until the tomatoes reduce to a mush. Stir in the chicken broth, wine, herbs and the Worcestershire sauce. Return the chicken to the pan and simmer for about an hour. Add the red pepper and zucchini for the last 20 minutes of cooking. Add water if necessary to maintain a gravy-like thickness to the sauce. Serve with rice or potatoes, salad and plenty of good, fresh bread.

Pasta Sauce

FATHER PETRI'S

It's fitting that my mom got this recipe from a family friend who claimed to have got it from a priest. It's truly a heavenly experience! Apparently he said it was divine intervention that makes the difference. I suspect it's the little extras that many people omit, like the sugar, Worcestershire sauce and the red wine. Or maybe it's just the wine! *Makes 4 generous servings*

INGREDIENTS

2 tbsp	olive oil
1	large onion, chopped
1	large clove garlic, minced or crushed
8 or 10	mushrooms, sliced
1	medium carrot, grated
1 lb	lean ground beef
2 or 3	hot Italian sausage links, split
2	large tomatoes, chopped
1 tbsp	oregano
1 tbsp	sweet basil
1/4 tsp	fennel seed (optional)
1	bay leaf
1 tbsp	sugar
2 tbsp	Worcestershire sauce
black pepper to taste	
salt to taste	
1	14 oz can tomato sauce
1 cup	red wine
1	small zucchini, sliced
1	medium sweet pepper, chopped

METHOD

Place 1 tablespoon of olive oil in a large skillet. Over medium heat, sauté the following: chopped onion, minced garlic, sliced mushrooms and grated carrot. Stir often to prevent burning. After 2 to 3 minutes add the ground beef and sausage meat. When cooked through, remove to a large pot. Add the rest of the olive oil to the skillet and sauté the tomatoes, oregano, basil, fennel, bay leaf, sugar, Worcestershire sauce and a pinch or two of salt and black pepper. When the tomatoes have disintegrated to a bubbling mush (about 4 to 5 minutes), transfer to the large pot. Place the pot over medium/low heat and add tomato sauce and red wine. Simmer for 10 minutes, stirring occasionally. Taste and add more salt and black pepper if needed. Add the zucchini and chopped sweet pepper. Simmer for 15 to 20 minutes. The sauce should have the consistency of a very thick gravy. If too thick just add a little water. Serve over your favourite pasta (follow directions on package).

Paella

This is probably the most well known of all Spanish dishes. It's a delicious blend of rice, chicken, sausage and seafood, all brought together with the unique taste of saffron. This last ingredient is the Rolls Royce of spices, at least 10 times more expensive than the next most expensive spice (vanilla beans). Saffron comes from the dried stigmas of the saffron crocus. It's harvested by hand and it takes 5,000 to make 1 ounce. Don't worry, you only need a pinch or two for a meal, for which you'll pay 50 cents to a dollar for a little pouch of powder or several dollars for a gram's worth of whole stigmas. It's not widely available, but can be found in Indian, Mid-eastern and gourmet food shops and delicatessens.

Serves 4

r e c i p e

2 tbsp	olive oil
4	chicken pieces
4	links of sausage (chorizo, hot Italian or another spicy type)
1	large onion, chopped
2	cloves garlic, crushed or minced
2 cups	white rice
1/2 cup	peas (fresh or frozen)
4 1/2 cups	chicken stock
1 tsp	oregano

a few pinches of saffron
(or substitute about 1/2 tsp of turmeric)
black pepper

8 to 12	jumbo shrimp, shelled
8 to 12	clams or mussels in shell
1	red or green pepper, cut in strips

lemon juice

METHOD

Preheat oven to 350°F. Put olive oil in a large skillet. Over medium/high heat sauté chicken and sausage until brown on all sides. Add onion and garlic. Reduce heat to medium-low and cook another 4 to 5 minutes. Stir in rice, peas, chicken broth, oregano and saffron. Add black pepper to taste. Cover the pan, bring to a boil and then reduce heat to a simmer for 15 to 20 minutes or until rice is done. There should be some liquid remaining on the bottom. If not, add a little more stock.

Remove from the heat and arrange the seafood and peppers on top of the rice. If your skillet doesn't have a metal handle, transfer the rice to an ovenproof casserole dish and then arrange seafood. Bake uncovered for 15 to 20 minutes, or until clams or mussels open. Drizzle with lemon juice and serve. Excellent with a nice, cold Spanish rosé.

THE MAIN EVENT

Veggie Pasta Sauce

The Italians love their vegetables. While I confess to being a shameless carnivore, I'll also admit there are times when a vegetable-based sauce is a nice, light alternative to a heavier meal. This is especially true when the weather is hot and humid. Of course one of the best things about this sauce is that it's incredibly good for you. Feel free to add any veggies you want to this one.   *Serves 4*

INGREDIENTS

2 tbsp	olive oil
2	large onions, peeled and chopped
1	large carrot, grated
10 - 12	mushrooms, sliced
2	cloves of garlic, peeled and minced or crushed
4	tomatoes, chopped
1 tbsp	oregano
1 tbsp	basil
1	bay leaf
1 tbsp	fresh chopped parsley
½ tsp	salt
½ tsp	fresh ground black pepper
1	8oz can tomato sauce
1 cup	red wine (use white if you want a more delicate sauce)
1 tbsp	sugar
1	medium-sized zucchini, sliced
1	green pepper, seeded and chopped
1	red pepper, seeded and chopped

METHOD

Heat the olive oil in a large skillet. Sauté onion, carrot, mushrooms and garlic until tender. Add tomatoes, and continue cooking until they begin to break down. Mix in the oregano, basil, bay leaf, parsley, salt and black pepper. Allow to cook for another couple of minutes. Stir in the tomato sauce, wine and sugar. Simmer for about 5 minutes and then add the zucchini and red and green peppers. Simmer covered for 10 to 15 minutes. The zucchini and peppers should be hot but still firm.

Serve over your favourite pasta: spaghetti, vermicelli, penne, etc. Or serve over a stuffed pasta like tortellini or ravioli. Top with Parmesan cheese. Don't forget the good bread and a nice glass of red wine.

This is one of my favourite meals when it's cold and miserable outside. It's an untraditional approach to a very traditional stick-to-your-ribs kind of meal. The traditional recipe calls for ground lamb. For some people, lamb is an acquired taste. Ground lamb can also be hard to find. If you can't get it or your guests don't like it, just use ground beef. *Serves 4*

Shepherd's Pie

method

Peel, slice and then boil the potatoes for 15 to 20 minutes. Check with a fork at the 15-min. mark. You don't want the potatoes to get too mushy! Mash with the butter and a pinch of salt until smooth. Cover and set aside. Put the oil in a large skillet. Over medium-low heat, lightly saute the onion, celery and carrot. Gradually add the ground meat. Add the cloves, basil and pepper. Occasionally stir the mixture as it cooks. When the meat is cooked through, add the beef broth, Worcestershire sauce and the corn. Taste the mixture. If you think it's needed add a little salt. Stir in the flour paste by the tablespoon until the sauce reaches a thick consistency. Pour the mixture into an 8 x 8-inch casserole dish. Spread the mashed potatoes evenly on top to the edges of the dish. Make a crosshatch pattern on top with a fork. Sprinkle lightly with paprika. Bake at 350°F for 30 to 40 minutes, or until the potato is lightly browned on top.

INGREDIENTS

4	medium-sized potatoes, peeled, boiled and mashed
2 tbsp	butter or margarine
2 tbsp	oil
1	large onion, peeled and chopped
1	stock of celery, sliced
1	large carrot, scrubbed and sliced
1-1½ lb	of ground lamb or beef
¼ tsp	ground cloves
½ tsp	basil

ground black pepper to taste

1½ cups	of beef broth
3 tbsp	Worcestershire sauce
1	small can of corn kernels

salt to taste (If using commercial bouillon cubes be very cautious about adding salt!)

¼ cup	flour paste

paprika for sprinkling

COQ AU VIN OR BOEUF BOURGUIGNON

These could very well be the perfect dishes. They're unbelievably delicious and never fail to impress, but are easy and cost effective. Both dishes sound exotic and romantic, yet they use a simple method of stewing meat in a savoury wine sauce. These two recipes go hand in hand because they are basically chicken and beef versions of the same French peasant dish. They make the most of simple ingredients and techniques.

Makes 4 servings

INGREDIENTS

1½ lb	boneless chicken breast or of stew beef or sirloin steak, chopped into bite-sized pieces
	flour or fine bread crumbs
3 tbsp	olive oil or butter
3 - 4	slices bacon, chopped
3	cloves of garlic, peeled, crushed or minced
1	large onion, chopped
10 - 12	large mushrooms, sliced thick
12	pearl onions, peeled (if you can get 'em fresh, if not just add another chopped onion)
	baby carrots, sliced (optional)
4 oz	brandy (optional)
1 tsp	sweet basil
1 tsp	marjoram
¼ tsp	sage
	black pepper to taste
12 oz	chicken (or beef) stock
12 oz	red wine
	a few dashes of Worcestershire sauce

METHOD

Coat chicken or beef in flour. Over medium to high heat, brown the meat lightly in the olive oil or butter. Remove to a plate. Sauté bacon, garlic and all veggies. When the onions are golden, return the meat to the skillet. Reduce heat to medium-low. Douse with the brandy and flame with a match. (This stage is optional but adds a richness to the flavour...and it's impressive and fun too!) When the flame dies, add the basil, marjoram, sage and pepper. Allow the juices in the pan to reduce and the veggies to brown a bit more. Don't let it burn!

Add chicken or beef stock, red wine and Worcestershire sauce. Simmer uncovered for about half an hour. Allow sauce to reduce to a gravy-like consistency. If it doesn't seem to be thick enough, mix in about a tablespoon of roux or flour paste (see section on thickening).

Serve with boiled or mashed potatoes, your favourite steamed vegetable and plenty of good bread to get that wonderful sauce.

This traditional "Olde English" dish seems to have been an "Olde Favourite" almost forever. For good reason. It's deliciously savoury, filling, good for you and gives the house a wonderful aroma. The traditional pie is topped with a piecrust (hence the name), but you can also use mashed potatoes if you want.

Makes 4 servings

Chicken Pot Pie

INGREDIENTS

Topping
Basic pastry crust
Follow the instructions in the section called "A Few Basic Recipes" in Chapter 2.

FILLING

1 lb	boneless, skinless chicken (cut into bite-sized pieces)
2 tbsp	oil
1	large onion, chopped
1 cup	chopped celery
1 cup	chopped carrot
1	clove of garlic, crushed or minced.
1 tsp	rosemary
1/2 tsp	tarragon
1 tsp	thyme
black pepper to taste	
1 cup	chicken stock
1 cup	white wine
1/2 cup	peas (fresh or frozen)
1/2 cup	corn kernels (ditto)
2 tbsp	flour
2 tbsp	butter

METHOD

In a large skillet, sauté chicken in the oil over medium heat until browned. Add onion, celery and carrot and sauté for about 5 minutes. Add garlic and cook for another 3 to 4 minutes. Add rosemary, tarragon, thyme and black pepper. Stir in the stock and the wine and bring to a low boil. Add peas and corn. Reduce heat to a simmer. Make a roux with the flour and butter (see section on thickening) and stir into the mixture. When it reaches the consistency of a thick gravy, transfer to a baking dish.

Preheat the oven to 350°F. Cover the dish with the pastry crust and crimp around the edges. Trim off the excess. Make a couple of slashes on the top to release steam during cooking. Bake for about 30 minutes or until pastry is golden.

Alternatively, you can use a mashed potato topping similar to shepherd's pie. Follow the mashed potato recipe found in the "Staples" section. Spread potato evenly over the chicken mixture. Make a crosshatch pattern on top with a fork. Sprinkle with salt and pepper and bake for 20 to 25 minutes or until topping gets a little golden.

Salmon is the king of fishes. One of my favourite meals is a beautiful salmon filet, poached or grilled. It's great with a salad or rice on a hot summer day. If cooked properly, it's so moist and delicious it doesn't need any sauce at all. The addition of ginger may sound a bit weird but trust me, it's fantastic!

Serve 1 fillet per person

Ginger*Salmon*

INGREDIENTS

1 tsp	soy sauce
1 tsp	fresh grated ginger (or ½ tsp powder)
2 tbsp	lime juice
1 tbsp	white wine or rice wine
1	salmon filet per person (use steaks if you can't get filets)

METHOD

Mix the first four ingredients. Marinate salmon in the sauce for about 30 minutes. In a large skillet bring about half an inch of water to a boil. Add a few ounces of wine and a squirt of lime juice to the water. Place the salmon in the skillet and reduce heat to a simmer. Cover and cook for 8 to 10 minutes.

This dish can also be broiled or grilled. Place the marinated salmon on an oiled rack and cook over medium-high heat 4 to 5 minutes per side. On the barbecue, cook it skin side down (or on a piece of foil) over low heat with the lid closed for about 8 to 10 minutes. You can baste periodically with the marinade or a squirt of lime juice.

My mother got this Hungarian recipe from a neighbour about 35 years ago. Giselle and her husband, Peter, escaped from Hungary during the 1956 uprising. My mom says she was one of the best friends she ever had, and certainly the best cook she ever met. Unfortunately, good paprika is hard to find, so Mom jazzed up the original recipe with some additional ingredients.

Makes 4 large helpings

Giselle's
Chicken
Paprikash

INGREDIENTS

¹/₄ cup	flour
4	chicken quarters or boneless, skinless breasts (for the health conscious)
2 tbsp	oil
1	large onion, chopped
3	large tomatoes, chopped
1	clove garlic, minced or crushed
2 tbsp	paprika
1 tsp	basil
1 tsp	marjoram
1 tbsp	sugar
1 cup	white wine
1 cup	chicken stock
1	green pepper, cut into strips
salt and black pepper to taste	
2 tbsp	butter
¹/₂ cup	sour cream

Chicken Paprikash

METHOD

Put flour in a paper bag. Shake chicken pieces in the bag to coat them. Heat a large skillet (medium-high) and add the oil. Sauté chicken to seal it and reduce heat to moderate. Add onion and cook for another 5 minutes. Add chopped tomato, garlic, paprika, basil and marjoram. Cook until tomatoes become mushy (about 5 minutes). Stir in sugar, wine and stock. Bring mixture to a boil, cover and reduce to a simmer. Cook for 20 minutes. Remove cover, then add green pepper and allow to cook for another 10 minutes to reduce the sauce. Make a roux with the butter and 2 tablespoons of the flour and stir it in to thicken the sauce. Mix in the sour cream. Serve over egg noodles or rice.

Chicken Parmigiana is another one of those dishes that sounds fancy and kind of romantic, but is amazingly simple. In fact, this is the nature of most Italian food: delicious food that's easy to make. Sounds perfect.

Makes 4 servings

Chicken Parmigiana

INGREDIENTS

1	egg, beaten
1	cup fine bread crumbs
4 tbsp	olive oil
4	boneless, skinless chicken breasts
1	onion, diced
1	clove garlic, crushed or minced
1	large tomato, chopped
1 tsp	oregano
½ tsp	basil
½ cup	red wine
8 oz	tomato sauce
1 tsp	sugar
1 cup	mozzarella cheese, grated
½ cup	Parmesan cheese, grated

METHOD

Beat the egg in a bowl. Spread bread crumbs on a plate. Over medium heat put the olive oil into a large skillet. Dip the chicken in the egg and then coat it with the bread crumbs. Fry chicken for 4 to 5 minutes per side. Be careful not to burn it. Remove to a plate. Add the onion to the pan and cook for 2 to 3 minutes. Add the garlic and cook briefly. Add tomato, oregano and basil and cook for about 5 minutes, until tomato disintegrates. Stir in the red wine and tomato sauce and sugar. Allow mixture to cook for another 5 minutes.

Meanwhile, preheat the oven to 350°F. Place chicken breasts in a baking pan. Space the pieces an inch or two apart because the cheese will run and you want to make sure the pieces remain as individual servings.(If you want, you can put each breast on a slice of bread. This will absorb some of the fat from the cheese during baking. Discard the bread before serving.) Cover each breast first with the tomato sauce, then with the mozzarella and finally with the Parmesan. Bake at 350°F for 20 to 30 minutes.

SWEET & SOUR
Meatballs

Another home favourite of mine. The only difference between mine and Mom's is that I make little baby meat patties instead of meatballs. Why? Simple: they brown easier and cook faster so you can eat sooner.
Makes 4 servings

1½ lb	ground beef
½ cup	fine bread crumbs
1	small onion, minced
1	egg
1 cup	brown sugar
⅓ cup	white vinegar
1 cup	tomato sauce
1 tbsp	oil

METHOD

Mix together the ground beef, fine bread crumbs, minced onion and egg. When thoroughly blended, form into small meat patties 3 to 4 inches in diameter and 1 inch thick. You should end up with about a dozen.

Mix the brown sugar, vinegar and tomato sauce until the sugar is dissolved.

Heat the oil in a large skillet. Brown both sides of the meat patties over medium heat. When nicely browned, pour the sauce over the patties. When the sauce begins to boil, reduce the heat, cover the skillet and simmer the patties for about 20 minutes. Serve with rice.

Sunday Glazed Ham

The sweet smell of glazed ham was something I always looked forward to on a cold evening after a hard day of tobogganing and snowball fighting. Of course, you can serve it any day you want.
Makes 4 servings

METHOD

Preheat the oven to 350°F. Mix the brown sugar, vinegar, dry mustard and cloves in a bowl or measuring cup. Place the ham slices in a shallow baking dish. Generously coat the ham slices with the glaze mixture. Bake uncovered for about 45 minutes. This dish is excellent with mashed potatoes and a side dish like ginger turnip or baked squash.
Makes 4 servings

INGREDIENTS

1 cup	brown sugar
¼ cup	cider vinegar
2 tsp	dry mustard
½ t	ground cloves or allspice
2 lb	ham (sliced about 1 in thick)

MEDITERRANEAN-STYLE HALIBU

Mediterranean food has so much to offer. Fresh vegetables, herbs, seafood and wine are just some of the bounty of the region. Here's a dish that combines many of these ingredients. Though halibut is an Atlantic fish, it's one of my very favourites. You could substitute almost any type of fish you like, but the cooking style is distinctly Mediterranean and could conceivably be found in any restaurant from Greece to Spain.

Makes 4 servings

INGREDIENTS

2 tbsp	olive oil
1	large onion, peeled and sliced
1	sweet red pepper, seeded and cut into strips
1	medium tomato, chopped
1	fennel bulb, cored and slivered
1/2 tsp	thyme
1/2 tsp	basil
1 tbsp	fresh parsley, chopped
1/4 tsp	each of salt and black pepper
1 tbsp	balsamic or red wine vinegar
2 tbsp	lemon or lime juice
1 cup	white wine
1 cup	water or fish stock
4	halibut steaks, about 1 in thick
2	lemons or limes, quartered for garnish

METHOD

Heat the olive oil in a skillet over medium heat. Add onion, red pepper, tomato and fennel and cook until onion is tender. Stir in thyme, basil, parsley, salt and pepper, vinegar, lemon juice, white wine and water or fish stock. Bring to a boil. Add the halibut steaks to the pan and spoon some veggies and liquid over them. Reduce to a simmer, cover and cook for about 15 minutes or until flesh is tender and flakes easily. Serve fish with some of the veggie mixture spooned over each piece. Garnish with lemon or lime wedges and a sprig or two of parsley.

I remember during my first trip to Europe eating lasagna in a small trattoria in Florence. What struck me, in my ignorance, was that it was served in small portions as an appetizer and was much simpler than many I had eaten back home. I didn't realize that Italians tend to eat large meals consisting of many small, individual courses. It's a wonderful and interesting way to eat. But I still like my lasagna as a main course with a salad and some nice crusty bread. What follows is a simple yet somewhat time-consuming recipe that's sure to please.

Makes 4 big helpings

Lasagna

METHOD

Start by making your pasta sauce. Make sure it's not too runny, or the lasagna won't hold together when it's served. Boil your lasagna noodles until almost done, 10 to 12 minutes. Assemble all your prepared ingredients and get ready to "build" your lasagna. Begin by spreading the olive oil and a little tomato sauce on the bottom of a baking dish (about 8 or 9 inches square and 4 inches deep). Cover the sauce with a layer of noodles (cut to fit). Top the noodles with about half of the remaining sauce. Spread half the ricotta cheese evenly over the sauce. Top this with half the mozzarella and a sprinkling of Parmesan. Another layer of noodles, followed by the remaining sauce and then ricotta. Now put the final layer of noodles, the rest of the mozzarella and a generous sprinkling of Parmesan.

Bake uncovered at 350°F for 40 to 45 minutes or until the cheese is golden and the noodles crispy around the edges. Remove from the oven and let stand about 10 minutes before serving. Serve with salad, bread and a delicious, slightly chilled Chianti or other Italian red wine.

If your first lasagna falls apart a little bit when you serve it up, don't sweat it... a little practice with the thickness of the sauce and you'll be just fine.

INGREDIENTS

1	recipe of Father Petri's Pasta Sauce or Veggie Pasta Sauce
2 tbsp	olive oil
8 -10	sheets of lasagna noodles (try spinach pasta, if you can get it)
1 lb	ricotta cheese (or cottage cheese)
½ lb	mozzarella cheese, grated or thinly sliced
¼ cup	Parmesan cheese, grated

ROCCO RAZZO

If I were to say I have a cooking mentor, it would have to be my good friend Mike Ingram. This guy is the natural goal scorer of the cooking world. He's one of those rare individuals that just have "the knack." Over the years I've learned a lot about cooking from him. The following recipe is one of my favorite Mikey dishes.

Serves 4

INGREDIENTS

3 tbsp	olive oil
1 lb	boneless, skinless chicken, thinly sliced
½ lb	jumbo to shrimp (peeled), or scallops
3	cloves garlic, minced
3	tomatoes, seeded and chopped (to seed a tomato, cut it in half and squeeze out the seeds and pulp)
a pinch of crushed chilies	
¼ cup	fresh chopped basil (or 1 tbsp dried)
1 lb	spaghettini or vermicelli, cooked
½ cup	grated Parmesan cheese

METHOD

Heat the olive oil in a large pan or skillet. Over medium heat, sauté the chicken. When done, add the shrimp (or scallops) and garlic and sauté for about 3 to 4 minutes (until shrimp turns pink). Add the chopped tomatoes, crushed chilies, basil and pasta. Toss the pasta in the pan with the other ingredients until hot. Add the Parmesan cheese and toss for about a minute until well mixed in. Serve immediately.

BOHEN

German food has to be one of the most misunderstood of all foods. Ja, Ja... sausage und sauerkraut. Well, the Germans sure do love their "wurst." But German food has a lot more to offer. Germany sits at the crossroads of Europe and has a wide range of influences on its cuisine. This recipe comes from the border region around Bavaria and Silesia and adds some spicy sweetness to the rather bland taste of pork. *Serves 4*

AN
hapsody

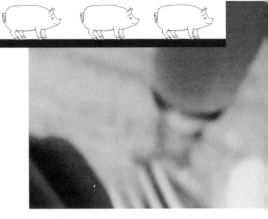

INGREDIENTS

1	pork chop per person (you can substitute or add bratwurst or knackwurst)
1 tbsp	oil
¼ tsp	salt
¼ tsp	black pepper
1	medium onion, chopped
¼ tsp	each of ground cinnamon, cloves, nutmeg
½ cup	lager beer
1	cup water
8	dried apple slices
8	dried apricots
8	dried prunes
3 tbsp	flour (for thickening)

METHOD

In a large skillet over medium heat, brown the pork chops (and sausage if using it) in the oil. Sprinkle with the salt and pepper. Add the onion and continue to fry. Stir in the cinnamon, cloves and nutmeg. When the onion becomes translucent, add beer, water, apples, apricots and prunes. Bring to a boil and then reduce to a simmer. Cook covered for about 30 minutes. Make a paste with the flour and some of the pan liquid or butter. Stir the mixture into the pan. When the sauce thickens, serve immediately. Excellent with mashed potatoes.

MONSTER
macaroni and cheese

Another traditional dish, macaroni and cheese is a recipe that varies from family to family. This one comes from my mom with my own variations thrown in. Chances are you'll end up doing the same.

Serves 4

INGREDIENTS

1¹/₂	cups elbow macaroni
6 or 8	mushrooms, sliced
1	small onion, diced
¹/₄ cup	green or red pepper, diced black pepper to taste
2 cups	grated cheese (use cheddar or try a mixture... Jarlsburg, Edam, Gouda, etc.)
3/4 tbsp	mayonnaise
6 oz	condensed cream of mushroom soup
1 cup	bread crumbs or croutons
¹/₂ cup	grated Parmesan cheese

METHOD

Boil macaroni about 7 minutes, until done but still firm. Drain and return to the pot. Add mushrooms, onion, green or red pepper, black pepper, cheese, mayo and condensed soup. Mix well. Pour mixture into a greased casserole dish. Sprinkle evenly with the bread crumbs or croutons and the Parmesan cheese. Bake in the oven at 350°F for 30 or 35 minutes. For a little twist try adding some canned tuna, chopped ham or cooked chicken.

MEXICAN
Tablecloth Stainer

This dish is one of those recipes that sound too weird to be true. The strange name comes from a special type of chili pepper traditionally used, called a "pasilla". This chili creates a dark red sauce, hence the name of the dish. I've never been able to find these potent little devils, and if you can't either, just use chili powder. It'll be delicious anyway.

Serves 4

INGREDIENTS

1 tbsp	oil
4	chicken breasts
4	large sausages (breakfast style, or use hot Italian or chorizo if you want)
1	large onion, chopped
1	clove garlic, crushed or minced
¼ cup	whole blanched almonds
¼ tsp	cinnamon
⅛ tsp	ground cloves or allspice
⅛ tsp	nutmeg
1 tbsp	chili powder
1 16 oz	can of tomato sauce
½ cup	of apple juice
1½ cups	chicken stock
Tabasco sauce to taste	
1	large apple, cored, peeled and sliced
1	large banana, sliced
½ cup	canned pineapple chunks, drained

METHOD

In a large skillet or Dutch oven, heat the oil over medium heat. Brown the chicken and sausage. Add the onion and garlic, reduce heat and cook until onion becom[e] translucent. Add the almonds, cinnamon, cloves, nutmeg and ch[ili] powder. Stir for a minute or so. Add the tomato sauce, apple juice chicken stock and several good shots of tabasco sauce. Stir and simmer covered for about 20 min. Stir in apple, banana and pineapp[le] and simmer for another 20 min. Adjust seasoning if necessary. Serve with rice and ice-cold beer.

THE MAIN EVENT

Chili con Carne

What needs to be said about this dish? It's delicious, easy, unpretentious and open to interpretation. Wow! I'm not sure what the hell I just said but it sounded good! Anyway, give it a try. The only essentials are meat, tomatoes, kidney beans and chili powder. The rest is up to you. It's great for an informal group or party. Try it with nacho chips or rice.

Makes 4 large serving

2 tbsp	oil
1 lb	ground beef
1	large onion, chopped
2	cloves garlic, minced or crushed
4	tomatoes, chopped
(or 1 16-ounce can stewed tomatoes)	
1 tsp	sugar
salt to taste	
1 tbsp	Worcestershire sauce
a few dashes of Tabasco sauce	
1 tbsp	chili powder
1 tsp	oregano
$\frac{1}{2}$ tsp	cumin
$\frac{1}{4}$ tsp	coriander
$\frac{1}{4}$ tsp	cayenne pepper
$\frac{1}{4}$ tsp	black pepper
1 16 oz	can red kidney beans
1 cup	tomato juice (or V8 juice)
1 cup	water

Serves 4 (large servings)

METHOD

Heat the oil in a large skillet. Fry the ground beef, onion and garlic until meat is browned. Add the chopped tomatoes (not the canned tomatoes if using them) and continue to cook until they begin to break down. Stir in sugar, salt, Worcestershire and Tabasco sauce and all herbs and spices. Allow mixture to fry for 2 to 3 minutes then add kidney beans, tomato juice, water and (if using them) canned tomatoes. When the mixture comes to a boil, reduce heat and simmer for 20 to 30 minutes. Allow liquid to reduce so the chili isn't too soupy. Note: You can add a variety of vegetables to this basic recipe. Try mushrooms, sliced zucchini, chopped red or green pepper, sliced green onion, etc. Try whatever you like.

Pastitsio

The Greeks have a knack for creating food that transcends the boundaries of east and west. Pastitsio provides us with a perfect example. The combination of lamb and pasta and the flavours of cinnamon and nutmeg are definitely reminiscent of the Middle East and times when the spice routes passed through Istanbul. This dish is great with a Greek salad.

Bring 6 cups of water and 2 tablespoons of cooking oil to a boil in a large pot. Stir in the macaroni and cook at a low boil for 7 to 8 minutes. Strain and reserve. Beat 2 eggs and ½ cup of Parmesan cheese together. Stir into the macaroni.

Meanwhile, heat the olive oil in a large skillet. Add the meat and onion and cook until meat is done and onion is tender. Stir in cinnamon, nutmeg, salt, black pepper, red wine and tomato sauce. Cover and simmer for about 15 minutes.

Spread ⅔ of the macaroni on the bottom of a greased 8 x 8-inch casserole dish. Cover with the meat sauce. Add the remaining macaroni. Bake uncovered at 325°F for about 15 minutes. Meanwhile, beat together the remaining three eggs, cream and Parmesan. Remove casserole from oven and pour on cream sauce. Sprinkle with some Parmesan cheese. Continue to bake uncovered for another 35 to 40 minutes or until topping is golden. Cut into serving-sized squares and chow down.

INGREDIENTS

6 cups	water
2 tbsp	cooking oil
2 cups	elbow macaroni
2	eggs, beaten
½ cup	grated Parmesan cheese

MEAT SAUCE

2 tbsp	olive oil
1 lb	ground lamb or beef
1	large onion, chopped
½ tsp	cinnamon
½ tsp	nutmeg
½ tsp	salt
½ tsp	black pepper
½ cup	red wine
1 8 oz	can tomato sauce

CREAM SAUCE

3	eggs, beaten
1 cup	light cream (10- 15 % milk fat)
1 cup	grated Parmesan cheese

MAKES 4 BIG SERVINGS

The Fantastic Stir-Fry

The stir-fry is fast, easy, delicious and very good for you. Not only that, but it's so versatile you can do just about anything you want with it. You can use chicken, beef, pork, shrimp, scallops, crab and a variety of vegetables to create a meal to suit your own taste. The important thing with a stir-fry is the method, not the ingredients. The cooking is fast, the veggies hot and crunchy, the meat juicy and tender. If you're serving this with rice, cook it first because the stir-fry takes less than 10 minutes.

Mix all sauce ingredients in a bowl. Prepare meat or seafood and marinate it in the sauce for about 15 minutes. Meanwhile, prepare all vegetables. When done, remove meat from marinade and reserve the liquid. Heat wok or large skillet over high heat. Add vegetable oil. When hot, add meat (or seafood) and stir frequently for 2 to 3 minutes. Add all veggies and continue to stir-fry (so that's where the name comes from!) for 4 to 5 minutes. Meanwhile, whisk cornstarch into a small amount of the reserved sauce. When well blended, add this to the rest of the sauce and pour the whole amount into the pan. Continue to stir until the sauce thickens. Serve immediately.

SAUCE

¼ cup	soy sauce
¼ cup	orange juice
2 tbsp	fresh grated ginger (or 1 tablespoon ginger powder)
2	cloves garlic, minced (¼ to ½ tsp garlic powder)
2 tbsp	rice wine (optional)
a few drops of sesame oil (optional)	
1 lb	of 1 of the following: - thinly sliced beef - thinly sliced boneless, skinless chicken - thinly sliced pork - scallops - jumbo shrimp, peeled - cooked crab legs, shelled and cut into bite-size pieces
1	large onion, sliced
1	green pepper, seeded and sliced
1	red pepper, seeded and sliced
1	head of broccoli, cut into bite-size pieces
1	large carrot, cut into thin, diagonal slices
1	medium zucchini, sliced
3 tbsp	vegetable oil
1 tbsp	cornstarch

SERVES 4

In case you haven't heard by now, pasta originated in the Orient. It was supposedly Marco Polo who brought it to Italy after one of his adventures to China. Here's a recipe that takes pasta back to its roots. Ginger roots, that is! The taste of seafood, curry and ginger are a delicious blend of flavours that puts a different twist on pasta. If you can't find vermicelli you can use spaghettini, spaghetti, linguini or whatever.

Singapore Vermicelli

Cook pasta by boiling about 3 times more water than pasta in a large pot. Add a little cooking oil and salt to the water and when it boils add the pasta. Bring back to boiling then reduce heat to medium low. Stir occasionally to prevent sticking. Cook vermicelli for about 5 mins. If using other pasta just follow directions on the package. Drain pasta when done.

Meanwhile, heat the oil in a large skillet or wok. When hot, add chicken and stir-fry for about 3-4 minutes. Add shrimp, garlic and ginger and stir-fry for about 2 mins. Add green onion, green and red pepper, mushrooms, pineapple and curry powder and continue stirring for another couple of minutes. Add oyster or teriyaki sauce, soy sauce and rice wine and stir for another 2-3 minutes. Add drained pasta and toss well. Serve when everything is mixed.

This recipe works equally well with pork, scallops, crab or even beef. You can also improvise on the veggies.

INGREDIENTS

Vermicelli pasta for 4
(see instructions on package)

4 tbsp	cooking oil
½ lb	boneless, skinless chicken, cut into bite-size strips
½ lb	jumbo or tiger shrimp, peeled
½ cup	green onion, cut into 1 inch pieces
1	red pepper, chopped
1	green pepper, chopped
8-10	mushrooms, sliced
½ cup	pineapple chunks (canned is okay)
¼ cup	slivered ginger (peel ginger root and cut into 1 inch slivers)
2	cloves garlic, minced
¼ cup	oyster or teriyaki sauce
2 tbsp	soy sauce
2 tbsp	rice wine (optional)
2-3 tbsp	curry powder

4 SERVINGS

the beautiful

Remember when burgers were a slab of ground beef, fried or grilled and topped with mustard and ketchup? You could call them pleb burgers. Not that I'm being snobbish about the poor old burger. I like them... really! It's just that there's so much more you can do with them. You can use ground beef, chicken, turkey or pork. Mix them with herbs, spices, chopped veggies, sauces, wine, etc. You can top them with just about anything and serve them on the traditional bun, bagels, tortillas, pita bread or whatever. One thing's for sure: burgers never need be boring again. It's a true dining renaissance and will change your life forever and...and... Okay, so I get a little carried away. Just have a look at the following ideas and then play around with them.

To make 4 quarter-pounders start with the following

INGREDIENTS

1 lb	of ground beef (hey, I'm a math whiz!)
1	egg, beaten
¼ cup	fine bread crumbs

Start with medium ground beef (referring to the fat content). This will produce nice juicy burgers. Mix all three ingredients together. Form into four equal patties. Don't mix or handle the meat more than is necessary and don't pack the patty together too tightly because it will end up drier. The bread crumbs and egg help to bind the meat together. The bread crumbs also retain moisture and fat to help keep the burgers from drying out. If health is a concern use lean meat and then mix in a little olive or canola oil. The oil is essential if using ground poultry.

Cook under the broiler for 4 to 5 minutes per side for a ¾-inch thick patty. You can also fry the burgers in a pan over medium heat for about the same length of time. Don't press down on the patty or poke it with a fork because it will release the juices from the inside and become drier. Ground meats should always be thoroughly cooked.

THE MAIN EVENT

...burger

BOEUF BOURGUIGNON BURGERS

1 lb	ground beef
2 tbsp	red wine
1 tbsp	Worcestershire sauce
¼ tsp	garlic powder
½ tsp	basil
½ tsp	tarragon
1	beaten egg
¼ cup	fine bread crumbs

salt and black pepper to taste

Mix ingredients, shape into patties and broil, grill or fry burgers as indicated above. Top with slices of fried bacon and sautéed mushrooms and onions. Serve in a nice fresh crusty roll or kaiser.

AZTEC BURGERS

Fantastic with an ice cold Corona, Dos Equis or Carta Blanca beer.

1 lb	ground beef
1 tbsp	chopped cilantro (or 1 tsp dried)
¼ cup	minced onion
2 tsps	chili powder
½ tsp	dry mustard
¼ tsp	cayenne pepper
1	beaten egg
¼ cup	fine bread crumbs

salt to taste

Prepare and cook as above. Top with melted Monterey Jack cheese or mozzarella and a spoonful of salsa.

TERIYAKI BURGERS

1 lb	ground beef
¼ cup	chopped green onion
1 tsp	ground ginger
2 tbsp	teriyaki sauce
1	beaten egg
¼ cup	fine bread crumbs

black pepper to taste

Prepare and cook as above. Top with a grilled pineapple slice and a thin spreading of teriyaki sauce on a toasted sesame bun.

BOMBAY BURGERS

You can use ground pork, lamb or chicken for these tasty morsels. Mix in with 1 lb of ground meat:

1 tbsp	curry powder
¼ cup	minced onion
¼ cup	raisins
¼ cup	slivered almonds
1	beaten egg
¼ cup	fine bread crumbs

Prepare and cook as above. Serve in a pita pocket or other flat bread. Top with Indian chutney (check out the gourmet or foreign food section of your grocery store).

CAJUN BURGERS

Turn up the heat and crank on some zydeco tunes.

1 lb	ground chicken or pork
1	small can baby shrimp or crabmeat
¼ cup	finely chopped red pepper (sweet or hot, it's up to you)
¼ cup	minced onion
2 tbsp	Louisiana-style hot sauce (or mix tabasco sauce with some ketchup)
1	beaten egg
¼ cup	fine bread crumbs

salt and black pepper to taste

Prepare and cook as above. Top with sliced tomatoes, peppers and some mayonnaise mixed with hot sauce or cayenne pepper. Serve in a toasted bun.

Old World Beef Stew

Beef stew sounds a little dull, but it's good, hearty food that sticks to your ribs and satisfies a serious hunger. The rich gravy and spicy warmth can really take the chill out of your bones on a cold, wet day. You'll probably serve it in soup bowls, but using a spoon or fork is up to you. Spoon or fork... the debate rages. Don't forget the bread.

INGREDIENTS

2 lb	stewing beef or thick, cheap cut of steak, cubed
⅓ cup	flour, seasoned with salt and pepper
3 tbsp	vegetable oil
2 lrg	onions, chopped
1 ½ cups	carrots, chopped
2 cups	potatoes, peeled and cubed
1 cup	turnip, peeled and cubed
1 cup	parsnip, peeled and sliced (optional)
3 cups	beef broth
½ cup	red wine (optional, but highly recommended)
1 tbsp	lemon juice
2 tbsp	Worcestershire sauce
2	bay leaves
¼ tsp	ground cloves
salt and black pepper to taste	

4 LARGE HELPINGS

METHOD

Coat the beef cubes in the flour and shake off excess. Heat a large skillet or heavy-bottomed Dutch oven over medium/high heat. Add oil and brown the beef on all sides (do it in batches so as not to overcrowd the pan). Add onion to the pan and cook over medium heat until they are tender. Place all the beef and onion in the Dutch oven (or a large pot if browning in a skillet).

Add lemon juice, Worcestershire sauce, bay leaves, cloves and some black pepper (start with about ¼ tsp). Pour in the beef broth and red wine and bring to a boil. Reduce heat and simmer covered for about 1 hour.

Add potatoes, carrots, turnip and parsnip and simmer for another 25 mins or until veggies are tender. Thicken sauce with a flour roux or paste if necessary. Serve in bowls with plenty of good bread or rolls.

THE MAIN EVENT

Baked Beans

Baked beans were something of a Saturday night tradition in our house. A cold winter night, baked beans with bacon and the Bruins and Canadiens on the TV. The aroma of beans slowly baking in the oven brings back great memories for me. You may not have any such history with beans, but one thing's for sure: they're incredibly simple to make. Oh ya... they're delicious too. This dish can be served as the main course or as a side dish with something like baked ham.

INGREDIENTS

1 cup	navy or small white beans (rinsed and soaked overnight in 2 cups cold water)
¼ lb	salt pork or thickly sliced bacon, chopped
1	lrg onion, peeled and quartered
1 tsp	dry mustard
¼ tsp	ground cloves
2 tbsp	brown sugar
2 tbsp	molasses
1 tbsp	Worcestershire sauce
½ tsp	salt
½ tsp	black pepper
½ cup	beer
1 cup	water

SERVES 4

82

THE JOLLY JOKER

METHOD

Heat 1 cup of water in a small saucepan. Add and dissolve the dry mustard, cloves, brown sugar, molasses, Worcestershire sauce, black pepper and salt.

Pre-heat the oven to 250°F. Place pre-soaked beans in a greased deep casserole dish. Mix in the salt pork pieces, onion, sugar/spice mixture and beer. Cover and bake for about 6 hours. Check the beans about once an hour to make sure they don't dry out too much. Just stir in a little water if you need to. The end product should be moist but not runny.

Serve with fresh bread, fried Canadian bacon or ham and a nice cold glass of dark beer.

chapter Six

Diversions

Side Dishes

Sometimes an interesting side dish can be just the thing to perk up a rather plain

main course. That doesn't mean a side dish has to be fancy and difficult to make.

Here's a bunch of recipes that are delicious and add a little something extra to a

meal without making things too difficult for the cook.

Heaven and Earth

The German version of mashed potatoes blends creamy potatoes with the spicy sweetness of applesauce. Sound a little weird? Give it a try and you'll see it lives up to its name. This recipe is very simple.

SERVES 4

4	large potatoes, peeled, quartered and boiled
3/4 cup	applesauce, preheated
2 tbsp	butter
1/4 tsp	cinnamon
1/4 tsp	nutmeg
1 tsp	sugar (optional)
1 tbsp	white wine vinegar (optional)

Mash the potatoes with the applesauce, butter, cinnamon and nutmeg. If you want a slight sweet n' sour tang, add a tsp of sugar and 1 tablespoon of white wine vinegar. Serve hot. Excellent with sausages or roasted meats.

Rasta Rice

There's no limit to the way you can jazz up rice. Play a little Bob Marley for inspiration.

MAKES 4 BIG SERVINGS

2 cups	rice
2 tbsp	oil
2	green onions, sliced
2	cloves garlic, minced
2 tbsp	fresh parsley, chopped
1/4 tsp	black pepper
1/4 tsp	cayenne pepper
1	bay leaf
1/2 tsp	coriander
1/2 tsp	cumin
2 cups	chicken broth
2 cups	water

In a large, heavy pot, briefly sauté the rice in the oil. Add the green onion and all the seasonings. Stir in the chicken broth and water and bring to a boil. Cover and reduce heat to a simmer. Cook for 20 minutes. Remove the cover and continue to cook until all the liquid is absorbed.

Try adding cubes of avocado or fresh grated coconut for the last 5 minutes of cooking.

aspAragusto

Asparagusto
Asparagusto
AspAragusto
Asparagusto
AspAragusto
Asparagusto

Parmesan Zucchini

If this doesn't make you think of sun-drenched Italy, nothing will.

SERVES 4

2 tbsp	olive oil
4	small zucchini (5 or 6- inches long), trimmed and sliced into thin medallions
1	medium onion, peeled and sliced into rings
10 -12	mushrooms, sliced
1	clove garlic, minced
½ tsp	salt
¼ tsp	black pepper
½ cup	Parmesan cheese, grated
1	8-ounce can tomato sauce
½ tsp	sugar

Heat the olive oil in a skillet over medium heat. Sauté the zucchini, onion and mushrooms for about 5 minutes. Add the garlic and cook for another minute. Add the salt and pepper and one half of the cheese. Mix well, then stir in the tomato sauce and sugar. Blend thoroughly and then pour the mixture into a casserole dish. Sprinkle with the remaining cheese. Bake at 350°F for about 20 minutes.

aspAragusto

There's something extra fancy about asparagus. When it's arranged artistically on a serving platter, it can help make a dinner very special indeed.

SERVES 4

1 cup	chicken stock
½ lb	fresh asparagus, stalks trimmed
1	sweet red pepper, seeded and cut in strips
¼ lb	thinly sliced prosciutto or cooked ham cut in 2-inch strips
	black pepper to taste
½ cup	hollandaise sauce (see sauces section above)

In a pan wide enough to allow asparagus to lay flat bring the chicken stock to a boil. Add asparagus and red pepper strips, and reduce heat to a simmer. Cook covered for 6 or 7 minutes. If you like your red pepper on the firm side, add them only for the last 2 minutes of cooking. Drain and arrange asparagus spears on a serving dish. Arrange red pepper and prosciutto strips near the middle of the dish. Top with sauce and sprinkle with black pepper.

Pulao

There are a variety of ways to make this rice dish that comes from India. It's usually made with cardamom, but this rather expensive spice can be hard to get. Use it if you want, but don't worry about leaving it out. Also, note the use of parboiled rice. In many dishes I find "sticky rice" is excellent. Not so with a rice dish like this. All the ingredients must mix well.

MAKES 4 SERVINGS

2 tbsp	butter
2 tbsp	oil
1 ½ cups	par-boiled white rice
¼ tsp	cardamom (if you can get it)
¼ tsp	cinnamon
¼ tsp	turmeric
3 cups	chicken broth
¼ cup	raisins
¼ cup	pine nuts
¼ cup	pistachio nuts, shelled

Heat the butter and oil in a large skillet or heavy-bottomed saucepan over medium heat. Add rice and sauté briefly until it's coated with the butter/oil and becomes glossy. Stir in the cardamom, cinnamon and turmeric and continue frying for a minute or so. Stir in chicken stock, raisins and nuts. When the liquid comes to a boil, cover and reduce to a simmer. Cook for about 20 minutes or until rice is tender.

Wickedly Delicious Baked Squash

I've never been a big fan of squash. But it does have two major things going for it: it's cheap and it's very good for you. So I figured I'd try to spruce it up a bit so I'd eat it more often. Give this a try... it's delicious and very easy.

MAKES 4 SERVINGS

1	acorn or butternut squash (approx. 6-inches diameter), quartered and seeded
1	large apple, peeled, cored and sliced
4 tbsp	brown sugar
	cinnamon
	nutmeg
4 tsp	butter

Make sure the squash quarters are well scraped out. Place them in a shallow baking dish, cavity side up. Put a slice or two of apple in each squash cavity. Sprinkle each with one tablespoon of brown sugar and a couple of dashes each of cinnamon and nutmeg. Top each one with a tsp of butter. Bake at 400°F for about 45 minutes or until tender.

They can be served "as is" or you can scoop out the contents onto each plate to simplify the situation at the table.

Ginger
turnip

Let's face it: there's nothing exciting about the poor old turnip. But they're very good for you and dirt-cheap. Here's a somewhat strange-sounding yet amazing way of preparing this neglected vegetable that'll make you want to eat it more often.

MAKES 4 SERVINGS

1 lb	of turnip, peeled and cubed
	small onion, minced
cup	chicken stock
1 cup	water
½ tsp	ground ginger
½ tsp	sugar
2 tsp	soy sauce

Combine all ingredients in a pot. Cover and bring to a boil. Reduce to a simmer and cook for about 20 minutes, or until tender. Drain and mash until smooth. Add a little butter and some of the drained cooking liquid if you want.

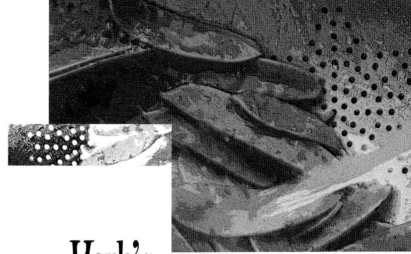

Herb's
Snow Peas

Snow peas are those little underdeveloped pea pods that you've probably had in Chinese food. Try this recipe and don't be afraid to experiment with different herbs. When you buy the snow peas make sure they're fresh and crisp.

MAKES 4 SERVINGS

1 tbsp	butter
1 tbsp	olive oil
½ lb	of snow peas, washed and trimmed
	a few pinches of salt
1 tsp	thyme (or another favourite of yours)
2	stalks of green onion, cut into ½-inch pieces
1 tbsp	fresh chopped parsley

In a large skillet, heat the butter and olive oil over moderate heat until butter melts. Add the snow peas, salt and thyme and cook, stirring occasionally, for 3 to 4 minutes. Add the green onions and parsley and continue to cook for another 2 or 3 minutes. Serve immediately

Green Beans with Orange and Nuts

Offbeat and delicious.

SERVES 4

1 lb	fresh green beans, washed and trimmed
2 tbsp	olive oil
1	small onion, peeled and cut into rings
¼ cup	unsalted cashews, almonds or pistachios
	salt and black pepper to taste
1	orange, sliced in half
1	tablespoon chopped parsley

Boil the green beans for about 5 minutes. Drain and rinse with very cold water.

Heat the olive oil in a large skillet over high heat. Add onions, cashews and season with salt and pepper. Sauté for 2 to 3 minutes, stirring frequently. Add green beans and squeeze orange halves into the pan (discard peel). Cook for another 2 to 3 minutes. Transfer to a serving bowl and sprinkle with chopped parsley.

CORFU TOMATOES

Greek food tends to be easy to make and very delicious. It's also different enough so that many people will never have had anything like it. This dish holds true to form. It's great for entertaining because it's delicious and fancy, yet surprisingly easy to make.

SERVES 4 PEOPLE

4	large tomatoes
	salt, pepper and sugar to taste
4 tbsp	olive oil
1	onion, peeled and finely chopped
½ cup	rice
¼ cup	pine nuts or pistachios (shelled)
¼ cup	raisins
2 tbsp	lemon juice
¼ cup	chopped parsley
½ tsp	chopped mint
1 cup	water

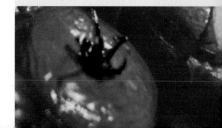

CorFu
ΤομΛτοΣς

Slice the top off each tomato (save the tops). Gently scoop out the pulp and reserve. Sprinkle the insides with a little salt, pepper and sugar.

Heat 2 tbsp of olive oil in a pan. Add the onion, rice and nuts and sauté for a minute or so until the rice becomes translucent. Add the tomato pulp, raisins, lemon juice, parsley and mint. Stir well, then mix in the water. Bring to a boil then reduce to a simmer and cook, covered, until water is absorbed (about 15 minutes). If rice isn't tender, add a little water and cook a bit longer.

Stuff each tomato with the rice mixture. Replace the tomato tops. Arrange in a baking pan and drizzle with remaining olive oil. Add about 1 cup of water to the pan. Bake at 350°F for about 30 minutes.

SIDE DISHES

For the Health of It: Salads and Dressings

Some people serve salads before a meal, others with the meal, and in Europe a salad is often served between the main course and the cheese or dessert. I prefer to serve it as a side dish. I said before that I wasn't going to devote much time to recipes for raw foods. I stand by that. But I thought it was a good idea to give you a little direction when it comes to salads n' such. Hey, we're all trying to eat a little healthier these days. You can always just buy some of your favourite veggies and top them with a store-bought dressing. That's passable most of the time. But if you want something a little special, try the following ideas.

salad NIÇOISE

This salad is popular all over the south of France. They even transform its basic ingredients into a sandwich. The essentials are tomatoes, black olives, boiled eggs and tuna. It's truly delicious and has the wonderful feel of the sun-drenched Mediterranean coast.

Makes 4 big servings

RECIPE

DRESSING

½ cup	olive oil
¼ cup	red wine vinegar
1 tbsp	chopped fresh basil (or 1 teaspoon dried)
1 clove	garlic, minced
salt and black pepper to taste	

SALAD

2	large tomatoes, cut into wedges
½ cup	black olives
2	green onions, sliced into ½-inch lengths
½	cucumber, peeled and sliced
1	green or red pepper, seeded and sliced
1 cup	green beans, cut in bite-sized lengths
2	large potatoes, cooked, peeled and diced
1	small can chunk tuna, drained
3 to 4	anchovy fillets, minced
1	head of romaine lettuce, broken into pieces
4	hard-boiled eggs, peeled and quartered

METHOD

Whisk together all the ingredients for the dressing. If using dried basil, allow the mixture to sit for at least 15 minutes.

In a large serving bowl combine the remaining ingredients, except for the eggs. Add the dressing and toss. Garnish with the egg quarters and serve. Fantastic on a summer afternoon with a chilled white wine or rosé.

Oriental-style
Vinaigrette

BEAT TOGETHER THE FOLLOWING:

3 tbsp	hoisin or oyster sauce
1 tbsp	freshly grated ginger (1 tsp powder)
1	large clove garlic, minced fine
a few drops sesame oil	
2 tbsp	rice vinegar (use ordinary white vinegar if you can't get it)
1 tbsp	lime juice
½ cup	water

This dressing goes well with lots of different vegetables, but try it with veggies that have an Oriental flair: broccoli, snow peas, sprouts, bok choy, peppers, water chestnuts and maybe some cold cooked chicken chunks or squid rings.

This is my ultimate salad dish. Fresh veggies, aromatic herbs, tart vinegar, feta and olives comb[...]
to create a fantastic taste sensation. It's great any time but especially on a hot summer day.

Makes 4 big servings

Greek Salad

INGREDIENTS

4	ripe, firm medium tomatoes (baseball size), chopped bite sized
1	medium onion, chopped
1	cucumber, halved and sliced
1	small green pepper, seeded and chopped
1	small red pepper, ditto
6 oz	black olives
$1/3$ lb	of feta cheese, broken into small chunks

DRESSING

$1/2$ cup	olive oil
3 tbsp	red wine vinegar
1 tbsp	oregano
1 tbsp	fresh parsley, chopped
1 tbsp	fresh mint, chopped

METHOD

Soak chopped onion in cold water for 15 minutes. Drain. Combine veggies, olives and feta in a large bowl and toss together. Whisk together the olive oil and vinegar. Add the herbs to the salad and pour the dressing on top. Toss and chow down.

Note: If you can't get fresh herbs use dried, but reduce the amount of each herb by half. Allow the herbs to soak in the oil and vinegar dressing for about 15 minutes before adding to the salad.

pasta *salad*

Pasta salad seemed to be a bit trendy for a while. Well, don't hold a grudge against it. It's good, versatile, open to personal whim and can be made well in advance. Great for barbecues, lunches, light suppers, etc. The following recipe is a bit bigger than my standard "Serves 4". This is because it keeps well and is so good for snacks and lunches to take to work or school.

Serves 4 (plus)

PREPARE AND COMBINE THE FOLLOWING:

4 cups	cooked pasta (any kind you like)
1	large stalk celery, sliced
4	stalks green onion, cut in 1-inch pieces
1	green or red pepper, seeded and chopped
¼ cup	pitted black olives, sliced
2 tbsp	fresh chopped parsley
1 cup	mayonnaise
½ tsp	fresh ground black pepper
½ tsp	salt

METHOD

You can add all kinds of things to this basic recipe. Try any vegetables (or fruit) that you like to eat raw: broccoli, cauliflower, carrot, snow peas, apple, etc. You can also add canned tuna, salmon, chopped cooked ham or chicken. To create a different taste, add one of the following: ¼ cup Parmesan cheese, 2 teaspoons of curry powder, a tablespoon of Dijon mustard, or a teaspoon of paprika.

Remember that if you increase the amount of dry ingredients like veggies or canned fish, etc. you have to increase the amount of mayonnaise accordingly. Use your judgement, adding the mayo gradually until you get the consistency you like.

Marie's Mother's Norwegian Potato Salad

There's something about potato salad that says "summer." It also says sunshine, barbecues and beer. Personally, I think it's great anytime of the year. It's easy to make and can stay covered in the fridge for several days. Make it in advance of a party or get-together to help take the pressure off being a host. This Norwegian recipe is delicious with the delicate sweetness of the apples and the zing of the onions.

Makes 4 large servings

INGREDIENTS

4	large potatoes
1	large onion, peeled and diced
2	large apples, peeled, cored and chopped
1 tbsp	lemon juice
1/2 tsp	salt
black pepper to taste	
2 tsp	white sugar
3/4 cup	mayonnaise

METHOD

Boil the potatoes for 20 to 25 minutes. Check their doneness with a fork. They should be firm. Allow them to cool, then peel and cut into 1-inch cubes. While the potatoes cook, peel and dice the onion. Place it in a bowl of cold water for 10 to 15 minutes. Peel, core and chop the apples. Place them in a mixing bowl and sprinkle them with the lemon juice. Drain the onions and add them and the potatoes to the apples. Mix in the salt, pepper, sugar and mayonnaise. Stir gently so as not to break up the potatoes.

Vinaigrette Dressing

Very simple, very good.

I'm not going to try to tell you what vegetables to use in your salad. You know what you like, what you have available and what you can afford. Let me just say that you shouldn't be afraid to experiment or try something new. If you're curious about some weird, new vegetable, ask the market guy or produce manager in the store what it's like or if you can have a little taste. They should have no objections since they want to expose people to these perishable products they're trying to sell.

Also, don't forget to be creative. In addition to vegetables you can also add things like cheese cubes, nuts, orange segments, strips of ham, chunks of tuna, slices of hard-boiled egg and a host of other tasty morsels limited only by your imagination.

To serve, you can either toss the veggies with the dressing just before serving or you can put the dressing in a separate bowl, bottle or whatever so that people can add it themselves.

BEAT TOGETHER THE FOLLOWING:

1 tbsp	Dijon mustard
2 tbsp	white wine vinegar
1 tbsp	lemon juice
1/4 cup	olive oil (extra virgin)
1 tbsp	finely chopped fresh parsley (not absolutely necessary)
salt and pepper to taste	

Serves 4

chapter 8

Save Some Room! Desserts

I've never been a big sweet eater. However, I know I'm definitely in the
minority. In fact, many people think I'm nuts (for lots of reasons!). Most people
love desserts. It's because of this that I couldn't just ignore what many people
feel is the perfect ending to a great meal. So what did I do? I asked Mom and a
few friends. What we came up with was a collection of delicious but very simple
recipes that are ideal for the beginner and for those who don't want a lot of fuss
in the kitchen. That's me!

Trifle

This is a very classy, fancy and traditional English desert that's perfect for small dinner parties. Mom gave me this recipe she's had for about 35 years.

MAKES 4 TO 6 SERVINGS

2 cups	of packaged custard or vanilla pudding
10	½ inch slices of store-bought pound cake
¾ cup	sherry (sweet)
½ lb	fresh or frozen strawberries or raspberries
½ cup	sliced almonds
1	large can sliced peaches
2	ripe bananas, peeled and sliced
2 tbsp	kirsch (cherry-based firewater)
1 ¼ cup	whipping cream

Make packaged custard or vanilla pudding according to directions on the package. Start with a large, clear glass bowl (part of the effect of this dessert is being able to see the trifle through the bowl). Put half of the pound cake slices on the bottom of the bowl (trim them to fit snugly and neatly). Sprinkle the cake with half the sherry. Top this evenly with half the berries. Layer in the rest of the cake and top with the almonds. Repeat the process with the sherry and berries. Now arrange the peach slices and then the banana slices over the berries and sprinkle with a few tablespoons of the peach juice. Spoon the custard or pudding over the top to a depth of about 2 inches. Now, beat the kirsch into the whipping cream until soft peaks form. Spread the whipped cream neatly onto the top of the trifle. Chill in the fridge until ready to serve. With something fancy-looking like trifle, always display it before serving it. It's silly to go through the trouble of putting it together if you can't reap the glory of how good it looks!

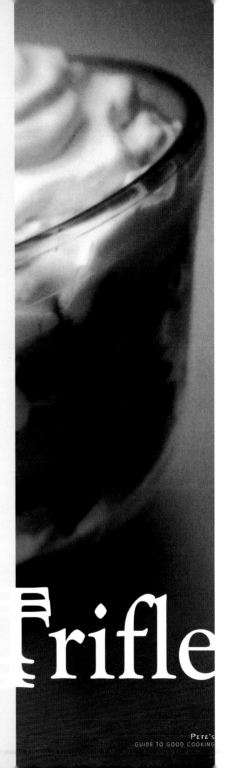

traditional perfect **Trifle**

Italian Ice Cream Balls

I had this in a small trattoria in Florence. It was fantastic... and that's saying a lot from someone who doesn't tend to go for sweets. My girlfriend had ordered it and when I tasted hers I had to get my own. I've expanded the concept to include a couple of variations. Pick one to suit your own taste.

SERVE AS MANY AS YOU WANT

Ice cream (vanilla or chocolate)
crushed almonds or hazelnuts
Amaretto (almond) or Frangelico (hazelnut) liquor

Start with very firm ice cream. You must be able to shape it into balls and roll it before it begins melting and running all over the place. A good way to do this is to make your balls with an ice cream scoop and put them back in the freezer as soon as you do each one. The size of the ice cream balls is really up to you. Obviously it's simplest to make them the size of your ice cream scoop. Once you have your balls made, you can begin phase two.

Spread the crushed nuts evenly over the surface of a dinner plate. Roll the balls one at a time in the crushed nuts. Press down gently but firmly to make sure the nuts stick. Be careful not to deform your ice cream. Re-freeze each ball as you finish it.

Serve straight from the freezer. Drizzle each ball with liqueur. Use Amaretto with almonds and Frangelico with hazelnuts. You can also top them with a little chocolate or caramel sauce and/or some whipped cream.

Man, you can really go nuts with this one. How about vanilla with pecans and orange liqueur... chocolate with walnuts and Bailey's Irish Cream...

BROWNIES

Here we go, the bad boy of sweets, the doom of dieters, the hitman of the dessert world. Brownies have always been popular in North America. Mothers have long used them to reward (bribe) their kids and husbands. Why are brownies so effective? It can be summed up in one word: killer!

MAKES 2 DOZEN (FEEDS ONE)

1 ½ cups	sugar
5 ¼ tbsp	unsalted butter
¼ cup	water
2 tsp	vanilla extract
3 oz	unsweetened chocolate, chopped
6 oz	semi-sweet chocolate, chopped
1 ½ cups	flour
½ tsp	baking soda
4	large eggs (room temperature)
1 cup	walnuts, chopped

In a large saucepan over medium heat, combine the sugar, butter and water and bring to a simmer. Stir in the vanilla and chocolate, and mix until the chocolate is melted. Set aside to cool until lukewarm.

Meanwhile, preheat the oven to 325°F and place a rack in the middle. Lightly butter a 13 x 9-inch baking pan.

In a small bowl, thoroughly blend the flour and baking soda (use a sifter if you have one).

When the chocolate mixture is lukewarm, beat the eggs (one at a time) into it with a spatula or wooden spoon. Gradually stir in the flour mixture and the walnuts.

Pour this mixture into the baking pan. Bake for 30 to 35 minutes. Test for doneness by inserting a toothpick. When it comes out with moist crumbs clinging to it, the brownies are done. Cool to room temperature before cutting. These can be served alone or with whipped cream or ice cream.

PEACH COBBLER

This is a down-home, country-style dessert that's been around forever. My mother said she got it at a woman's church group and that it definitely predates me. She makes it every summer when fresh local peaches are in the store.

MAKES 4 TO 6 SERVINGS

8 or 9	ripe peaches, sliced and pitted (or 2 large cans sliced peaches)
$\frac{1}{2}$ cup	sugar
1 tbsp	lemon juice
1 cup	flour
1 $\frac{1}{2}$ tsp	baking powder
$\frac{1}{4}$ tsp	salt
$\frac{1}{4}$ cup	milk
1	egg

Preheat the oven to 400°F. After pitting and slicing the peaches, you should have about 4 cups. Put them in a large bowl and mix with the sugar and lemon juice. Set aside. In a large mixing bowl blend the flour, baking powder and salt. Gradually stir in the milk until you have a nice sticky mixture. Mix in the beaten egg until combined. Butter and then fill a deep 8 x 8-inch baking pan with the peach mixture. Top this with the dough-like mixture. Spread it evenly, using your hands or a wooden spoon or spatula. Bake for about 30 minutes until the crust is golden and peach juice bubbles around the edges. Serve it warm with a little whipped cream or vanilla ice cream.

Fruit Compote

When I was growing up, my mother didn't always have the time or inclination to bake cakes, pies and such. Very often our dessert would be some type of fruit. Sometimes fresh, sometimes canned and sometimes with ice cream or whatever. Looking back, I see that this came largely from her desire to give her kids better eating habits.

MAKES ABOUT 6 SERVINGS

¹/₄ cup	water
¹/₂ cup	sugar
¹/₄ tsp	cinnamon
1/8 tsp	ground cloves
2 lbs	mixed fresh fruit, pitted, cored, peeled and sliced as needed (Use your imagination!)
3 tbsp	lemon juice
¹/₂ cup	fruit flavoured brandy or other liqueur

Bring the water to a boil and add the sugar, cinnamon and cloves. Reduce to a simmer and stir until the sugar dissolves. Prep all your fruit (do the apples and pears last because they'll start to turn brown quickly), place it in a large bowl and sprinkle with the lemon juice. Pour the sugar and spice liquid over the fruit and then add the booze. Mix well, but gently. Chill for about 2 hours, stirring periodically. Serve plain or topped with whipped or ice cream.

DESSERTS

Apple Brown Betty

I like cooking with apples. They're cheap, nutritious and delicious. I suppose my upbringing has a lot to do with it. We always had apples in the house and when my mother made dessert, she often used them. To me, Apple Brown Betty is real comfort food. This recipe is identical to Mom's except for the addition of the rum.

Sorry Mom, I couldn't resist!

MAKES 4 GOOD HELPINGS

1 cup	raisins
3 or 4 tbsp	rum (amber is nice)
5 to 6	tart apples, peeled and sliced
1 tbsp	lemon juice
1/2 cup	flour
1/2 cup	brown sugar
1/4 tsp	salt
1/2 tsp	cinnamon
1/4 tsp	nutmeg
4 tbsp	butter, chilled and firm
1/4 cup	walnut pieces
1 1/2 cups	coarse white bread crumbs
1 cup	apple cider (use juice if you can't get cider)

Preheat the oven to 350°F and butter a deep 8 x 8-inch baking pan.

Soak the raisins in the rum until most of it is absorbed. Toss the sliced apples with the lemon juice.

Mix the flour, brown sugar, salt, cinnamon and nutmeg. Add the butter and mix with a pastry blender until you have a coarse, mealy-type mixture.

Fill the baking dish with half the apples, half the raisins and walnuts and then top with half the flour mixture and bread crumbs. Add the rest of the apples, raisins and walnuts, then pour on the apple cider. Top with the rest of the flour mixture and breadcrumbs.

Cover the dish with aluminum foil and poke a few holes in it. Bake for 30 minutes. Uncover and continue to bake for another 15 minutes until golden. Serve warm. Top with whipped cream or vanilla ice cream. If you're feeling extra decadent, drizzle a little rum over each serving.

MAZERATTIS

This recipe was given to me by Dana, my old friend Ronnie's Polish-born stepmother. The real name is Mazurkas, but we always called them Mazerattis because they went so fast! Many traditional Polish recipes are very simple to make and use common ingredients. This one's no exception.

MAKES 3 DOZEN

1 cup	unsalted butter at room temperature
¾ cup	eggs, beaten (the number of eggs depends on their size)
2 cups	ground almonds
1 ¾ cups	flour
1 cup	sugar

Method:

With a spatula or wooden spoon, cream the butter and gradually beat in the eggs until fluffy. Combine the almonds, flour and sugar and gradually add this dry mixture to the butter/egg mixture, beating continuously.

Pat the dough into a greased baking pan (about 12 inches square is good). The dough should be about 1 inch thick. Bake at 350°F for about 20 minutes or until golden on top.

Spread with jam or drizzle with chocolate sauce and allow to cool. Cut into 2- or 3-inch squares and serve.
Great with ice cream.

Drunken Moose

Yeah, I know... it's really mousse. Who cares?

It's good anyway.

Certainly classier than electric Jell-O.

MAKES 4 TO 6 SERVINGS

1	small package orange or cherry-flavoured gelatin (3 ounces)
1 cup	boiling water
1/4 cup	cold water
1/4 cup	orange liqueur or cherry brandy
1 cup	whipping cream

Dissolve the gelatin in the boiling water. Stir in the cold water and cool to room temperature. Add the liqueur or brandy (don't add it until the gelatin mixture has cooled or all the alcohol will evaporate... God forbid!). Chill in the refrigerator until the gelatin starts to thicken (about 30 minutes). Don't rush it because if the gelatin is too runny it will separate when combined with the whipped cream.

Whip the cream until it forms soft peaks. Slowly fold in the gelatin. Stir gently until evenly blended. Pour into individual dessert cups... parfait-style is nice to use but you can also use large wineglasses or anything else clear and sort of fancy. Chill until set, 1 1/2 to 2 hours. Top with whipped cream, chocolate sprinkles, cherries or whatever.

Poached Pears with Chocolate Sauce

This is another gem from sunny Italy. You might think chocolate and pear is a bit of an odd combo. Not so. This is reminiscent of those little booze-filled chocolates that my brothers and sisters loved as kids.

SERVES 4

Poached pears:

3	cups water
¼	cup white sugar
4 tbsp	lemon juice
4	large, ripe, firm pears, peeled and cored
1 cup	cherry brandy

Chocolate sauce (1 cup):

½ cup	white sugar
½ cup	water
2 oz	baker's chocolate
1 tsp	vanilla

Mix the water, sugar and half the lemon juice in a medium-sized saucepan (about 2-quart size). Bring to a boil and stir to dissolve the sugar. Peel and core each pear. Make sure the bottoms are flat so the pear will stand up. As each pear is peeled, drizzle it with some lemon juice to help keep it from browning.

Add the cherry brandy to the boiling water and when it returns to the boil, add the pears. Reduce heat and simmer for 10 to 12 minutes. Remove the pears from the liquid. Allow to cool.

Meanwhile, in a small pot, dissolve the sugar in the water over medium heat. When thoroughly dissolved, allow to cook until a syrup develops (about 5 minutes). Gradually melt the chocolate into the syrup and stir in the vanilla. Mix until smooth and creamy. If the sauce is a little too thick to pour, just stir in a little more water (or try some cherry brandy). If you want to be a little quicker you can always use a sundae chocolate sauce that's semi-liquid at room temperature.

Gently pat the pears dry and drizzle them with generous amounts of chocolate. Refrigerate until ready to serve.

chapter 9

That's Entertainment!
Planning Menus: What Goes With What?

Okay, so in a brief moment of weakness, you invited a few people over for dinner. Maybe it's a date. Maybe it's another couple who've had you and your better half over to their place umpteen times, and you owe them big. Or maybe it's just a group of friends. The point is, now you've got to produce! What do you make? What's appropriate? Is there some kind of theme? How complicated should you get? Are your friends worth it? Is your date worth it!!?
Questions... questions...

Deciding on a menu can be a complex series of choices, based on an in-depth understanding of how different flavours work together to complement and contrast with each other. The goal is to create the utmost enjoyment in the dining experience. Professional chefs devote a lot of time and effort to figuring out what works and what won't.

So what are the rest of us poor amateurs supposed to do? Use a little common sense and the experience of others to help you along. After a while you'll develop your own knowledge and insight.

Conventional culinary practices generally stress balance and variety. You probably wouldn't serve chicken as an appetizer and a main course. You also probably wouldn't serve too many rich sauces with the same meal.

In fact, the idea of what goes with what is really open to debate. Various cultures have widely different views on planning meals. The notion that you can't serve something with something else is mostly the result of cultural snobbery and tradition. The bottom line is that if you think two dishes might go well together, go ahead and give it a try.

If you're unsure or unwilling to experiment, stick to a more traditional approach. Base your menu on one main dish that'll dominate the overall flavour of the meal, and then one or more side dishes that will play second fiddle. This will also make it easier for the beginner to plan a menu. Concentrate on the main dish and then make a couple of side dishes that won't complicate things too much.

A soup, salad or appetizer before the main course can stand more or less on its own. You don't need to worry too much about how this will affect the meal; in fact, a little variety is a nice way to make a menu more impressive.

The beginner should try to make a starter course that can be done in advance.

When planning your menu, remember that people see their food before they taste it. There's a reason people say, "Hey, that looks good enough to eat!" A pleasing appearance always enhances the overall impact of a meal. A nice mix of colours and the appropriate use of garnishes (lemon, lime or tomato wedges, orange slices, sprigs of parsley or other herbs) are simple ways of making food look great.

Nutrition should also play a role in menu planning. I'm no expert and I'm not going to try to tell you how to eat. But, a while back I took a night course on nutrition. The nutritionist who gave the course said that our diets should be based on grains and legumes and fruits and vegetables. Next on the list are dairy products and meats and fish. She said that variety is very important and it's the best way to ensure that we get healthy and well-balanced diets. The main things to be concerned about are your intake of fat (particularly saturated fats from meat, dairy products and nuts) and salt. As always, moderation is the best policy. Junk food and most restaurant foods are loaded with fat and salt. That's the simplest way to make food taste good, zesty and rich. When you cook at home using fresh and minimally processed ingredients, you have total control over what you eat.

Have a look at the following menu suggestions and use some common sense and your imagination when preparing your own. At first, keep it as simple as you can. Do as much in advance as possible. That way you won't be running around like a maniac when your guests arrive. People are really impressed by how you seem to have everything under complete control (hee, hee, hee). And don't forget to have fun.

THAT'S ENTERTAINMENT!

A Little Romance

Why go out and spend big bucks on a fancy dinner when you can stay home and impress her or him with your kitchen savoir faire? To make things go more smoothly, make the salad (keep the dressing on the side), chicken and dessert in advance, put the potatoes in the oven about an hour before dinner and get the snow peas prepped and ready to cook. Serve the salad as an appetizer while the potatoes bake and the chicken simmers. When the taters are done, turn the oven off and sauté the snow peas. When they're done, serve and impress! The ice cream balls can stay in the freezer until you're ready for them.

Salad Niçoise
~~~~~~~~
Coq au Vin with Baked Potatoes and Herb's Snow Peas
~~~~~~~~
French red wine like a Burgundy or Merlot
~~~~~~~~
Italian Ice Cream Balls

You and the Boys and Game Seven

Men, sports, beer and a steaming cauldron of food. All very primitive. Gotta problem with that?

Sinful Scallops
~~~~~~~
Chili Con Carne
or
Old World Beef Stew
~~~~~~~
Ice cold lager beer
~~~~~~~
Brownies

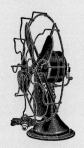

Hot Summer Night

It's hot and sticky and you don't know whether to drink your beer or pour it over your head. That's okay... get to the balcony or backyard and fire up the barbecue.

Greek Salad
or
Marie's Mum's Norwegian Potato Salad
~~~~~~~
Beautiful Burgers
or
Grilled Ginger Salmon
~~~~~~~
Ice cold beer and white wine (Sauvignon Blanc or Chardonnay or maybe a white Zinfandel)
~~~~~~~
Fruit Compote

Computer Crash

Got papers, exams or a little work from the office? Try this simple approach to feeding yourself during the dreaded "all-nighter." The soup gets better with age, so leave it to simmer and you can grab a bowl anytime you want.

Serbian Bean Soup
or
Pea Soup
~~~~~~~
Your favourite sandwiches
~~~~~~~
Lots and lots of coffee

The Big Night

Okay, now you've done it! You've invited a bunch of people over for dinner. I guess you shouldn't have been bragging about how good you're getting in the kitchen, eh? No matter. You can handle this, no problem. Do as much ahead of time as possible and try not to look like a crazed maniac when the guests arrive.

Greek Salad
~~~~~~~
Lasagne
or
Pastitsio
~~~~~~
Asparagusto
or
Corfu Tomatoes

Fresh bakery bread
~~~~~~
Slightly chilled Italian red wine
or
Cold Spanish or Portuguese Rosé
~~~~~~
Poached Pears

The Folks are Coming!

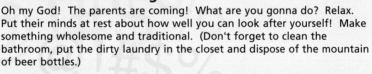

Oh my God! The parents are coming! What are you gonna do? Relax. Put their minds at rest about how well you can look after yourself! Make something wholesome and traditional. (Don't forget to clean the bathroom, put the dirty laundry in the closet and dispose of the mountain of beer bottles.)

Mixed Salad with Vinaigrette Dressing
~~~~~~~
Wickedly Baked Squash
and
Shepherd's Pie
or
Chicken Pot Pie
~~~~~~~
Apple Brown Betty

Conclusion

There's a vast and fascinating world of cooking out there to explore. I hope this book helps you on your way to becoming both a competent and a confident cook. Of course, there's much more to learn, but by mastering the basic skills and knowledge found in the preceding pages, you should be well prepared to venture out on your own.

Learn new things anywhere you can: cookbooks, friends and relatives. Don't be afraid to try new ideas you come across in restaurants or when travelling. Believe me, one of these days you'll look back and laugh because you thought you couldn't cook. You might even find yourself giving your Mom some cooking tips. Anyway, I hope you will enjoy cooking as much as I do. Good eating and have fun!